5 Tips
from
Jesus
for
Desperate
Parents

By Kia Hunt

5 Tips from Jesus for Desperate Parents

Copyright © 2021 by Kia Hunt

Roan Dog Publishing, LLC

ISBN: 9798488653795

Editing by Renée Gotcher, www. reneegotcher.com
Cover and interior design by Roan Dog Publishing, www.roandog.com
Cover photo by Anthony from Pexels
Interior photos by Karolina Grabowska from Pexels

For Roger

Glad to be traveling life with you.
You always make sure we have the passports.

Acknowledgments

Thank you to Doc Hunsley, not only for writing the foreword for this book, but for opening the door for me to teach this content as a small group Bible study many years ago at Grace Church. You envisioned this reaching a larger audience than I was able to imagine at that time, and you challenged me to think bigger. And to Kay Hunsley, you were kind enough to join my very first small group study. It was probably pretty rough back then. I hope it has improved with every group I've taught since. Thank you both for your support.

To every parent who has joined me in a 5 Tips small group Bible study over the years, thanks for letting me test-drive this material with you. Each of you have demonstrated what it means to love your children though every situation. You have taught me the joy of vulnerability in a community of Christ's followers. You have inspired me to continue on my journey to share Jesus's words to desperate parents. I still think of you often and pray that God is blessing your families.

Thank you to the individuals who shared their stories for this book. I hope anyone who reads your stories will be inspired to share their own journey with others. We need more desperate parents who are willing to take off the mask of having it all together and reach out to others who are struggling.

I am grateful for the family and friends who have walked alongside our family, praying with us through difficult times. Thanks for encouraging me to finish this project and for listening to me babble about it for years. Your consistent support means the world to me.

Thank you to my writing group—especially its founder Kelli Sallman. You always find the right balance of cheerleader and challenger to motivate and inspire. This eclectic circle of writers keeps me learning and laughing.

Thank you to Renée Gotcher for your writing advice and editing. This book is so much better due to your wealth of knowledge and helpful guidance. I'm so glad God connected us and hope there are future projects in store for us.

Caden, I am excited about the path you're on. I can see you maturing into a man who will take on challenges fearlessly but with wisdom. When I look at the gifts God has given you, and how you're using them for good, I know he has some amazing things planned for your life. I could not be more proud of you.

Contents

Foreword

by Stephen "Doc" Hunsley, MD

I am so excited that you have chosen to read *5 Tips from Jesus for Desperate Parents!* This book is a must-read for every parent, whether you are a parent of a child with special needs, a mental health disorder, a medically fragile child, or a neuro-typical child. I have had the privilege of knowing Kia Hunt for several years and talked with her about her dreams for this book in its early stages. I firmly believe in the biblical truths that Kia shares in this book. I encouraged her to teach this material as a Bible study for small groups. Now, as a book I'm thrilled to know that what she has to share can reach even more parents.

I can personally say I have been a "desperate parent" on more occasions than I can count. God blessed me with one son with special needs and both of my other two kids have ADHD. Many days I feel like I fail as a father. But my desperate parent story is one of depending on Jesus through my most difficult times to find he was always with me, guiding me where I needed to go.

Everyone calls me Doc, because I am a pediatrician who worked in a Pediatric Emergency Room and Urgent Care. I loved my job, but it almost killed me. I found I was very susceptible to the infectious diseases of my patients. One event put me in the hospital and ICU for 46 days. I was given less than .01% chance of survival. On three different occasions they told my wife I was not expected to make it through the night. But God had different plans!

I went through nine months of rehab just to be able to walk again, only to land back in the ICU from the flu. It was then they discovered that I am the only known person in the world to have a partial paralysis of the diaphragm—that's the main muscle that allows you to breathe. With only about 40% lung capacity I couldn't fight upper respiratory infections very well. Again, God had his hand on me and walked me through that struggle.

On my first day back to work my employer called me into a meeting. I walked into a room filled with every one of my supervisors, the entire HR department, two rows of attorneys, and a row of physicians I'd never met. I was guided to a single chair facing everyone in the room. They informed me that I had become a medical legal risk to the hospital. They were afraid that I would get sick again from one of my patients and die, and then my family could sue the hospital. At the recommendation of the gathered experts they determined that they would put me on long-term disability—immediately ending my medical career forever! Yes, that is correct, I had to hang up my stethoscope and never practice medicine again.

Before I move on, let me tell you more about my family. At the time of this writing, I have been married to my amazing wife Kay—also a pediatrician—for 26 years and we have three children. Our oldest son Luke is in college, and our youngest daughter Sarah is in middle school. Our second son Mark Andrew Hunsley is a big part of our desperate parenting journey. When he was eight months old, he had a seizure that lasted four hours. By 18 months old he was diagnosed with Dravet Syndrome, a rare genetic seizure disorder. By the time he was two, we got a second diagnosis of autism.

After losing my medical career, I took on the hardest job I ever had—becoming Mr. Mom for our two amazing boys! Through my work with children in the hospital I already had a special place in my heart for kids with special needs. My experience is that they have so much to offer and amazing love to give. Both I and my wife had a doctor's perspective of caring for children with special needs, but for the first time we actually understood what it meant to be parents of a child with special needs. We felt the immense stress, the stares when we went out in public, and experienced the grief of losing the dreams we had for Mark.

A few years later, I became a volunteer Children's Pastor at the church we attended and helped grow a Children's Ministry to have over 1,000 children. As a father of a son with special needs and knowing how important it was to be able to minister to them in specific ways, I went to our pastor and asked if I could organize a ministry for families like ours. He immediately said, "No Doc, we don't want those kinds of people here." My jaw dropped and I thought, time out, *I am* that kind of person. About a year later I was asked to create a small program for a few adults with disabilities who were disrupting the service— which I gladly did.

Then, on November 1, 2010, Mark was cured of his Dravet Syndrome and autism when he was born into Heaven at the age of five and a half. The only way we were able to cope was to face each day through the love of our Lord Jesus Christ. Shortly after that, I had another near-death health crisis. While recovering from both of those traumas God made it clear that our family needed to go to a different church. God led us to Grace Church in Overland Park, Kansas.

I have found that in order to heal—physically and emotion-ally—I need to serve. I bounce back quicker when I am helping others. After losing my career, my son, and the children's pastor position I loved, I couldn't wait to get back into service. I went to the leadership of our new church and said, "You got me! I'll do whatever you need." Their children's pastor immediately responded saying, "We've been praying for years about how to create a world-class children's ministry. The only way to do that is to have a special needs ministry. We believe God brought you here because you are the right person to create that."

We started small, but God blessed our efforts and allowed me to create SOAR (Special, Opportunities, Abilities, & Relationships) Special Needs Ministry. As the volunteer Special Needs Pastor at Grace Church for eight years, we grew the ministry to serve over 900 individuals in the Kansas City area.

As of December 2019, SOAR became an independent 501(c)(3) non-profit organization. I am the Executive Director and Founder. SOAR exists to empower families with disabilities to "soar" in their local and faith communities. We help answer the three main questions that every family with a child with a disability has:

1. Will my child ever be able to provide for themselves?
2. Who will take care of my child once I'm gone?
3. Who will take care of me?

SOAR serves individuals with special needs of all ages and severities. Our services include respite nights—that give parents an evening of relief, summer day camps, and the annual Wonderfully Made Special Needs Conference. We have also assisted over 320 churches in the United States, Canada, Brazil and Jericho to start or improve their special needs ministries.

Because of the spark Mark ignited, God has given us a vision for the future which includes:

• Starting one thousand special needs ministries in churches or organizations throughout the world in the next ten years!

- Building facilities to host respite services—allowing parents opportunities to recharge.

- Creating an Adult Job Training Center to provide guidance and training to teens and adults with disabilities to equip them for jobs they are passionate about.

- Providing adult assisted living and independent living environments that are safe and accommodating.

- Growing our advocacy program and counseling network for parents.

- Organizing mission trips for families with disabilities to serve other individuals with disabilities; because nowhere in the Bible does it say, only those with an IQ over 70 should "Go into all the world and share the gospel!"

To learn more about SOAR, visit SOARspecialneeds.org. Come SOAR with us!

The adversity of losing a child, two careers, and almost losing my life brought us many moments of desperation. But I am grateful for the journey. God used Mark's time here on earth to teach and prepare us to be able to minister to hundreds of other families, and to walk alongside them through the highs and the lows. I am more passionate today about serving families of special needs than I ever was about being a pediatrician.

The learnings Kia shares in this book from her journey resonate with our experience as parents as well. We can't understate the importance of relying on God through every challenge. The five tips mentioned in this book are evidence of Jesus's love and encouragement to parents.

For example, we have learned to deal with other people's stares and judgement with grace; we know—and are completely fine with the fact—that our normal is not the same as most others. God helped us realize the importance of advocating for our children—just like He advocates for us. We have learned to encourage our children's strengths and celebrate their successes. We practice faith as we pray for our children's future. We believe that, with God's help, our many years of prayer and investing in our children will produce a young man and woman who will make an incredible impact on society.

Perhaps most significantly to our family, we choose joy. We went through some dark days after the death of our son Mark. Kay and I could have chosen to be mad (and we were at first), but we changed our perspective. We look ahead to the day we will be reunited because we have made Jesus Christ our personal Lord and Savior! We found joy knowing he was no longer having seizures. We focus on the positive memories we have. This joy of remembering Mark and being thankful that God blessed us with him, even though short in time, has truly given us the "peace that passes understanding" that God promises in Philippians 4:7.

> The five tips mentioned in this book are evidence of Jesus's love and encouragement to parents.

I would do anything to have Mark here now, even if he was having another seizure or autistic meltdown; but I take complete comfort in knowing that this was all part of God's plan. Because God blessed my family with Mark, today I am filled with passion for families with special needs. Working endlessly to serve them fills me with complete joy. I am living out Mark's purpose! SOAR Special Needs is Mark's legacy and purpose.

My prayer as you read this book is that you will see that our children are a gift from God, they are created in the image and likeness of God, they are NOT a mistake! I pray you will learn how to navigate through life as a desperate parent. There is nothing wrong with being a desperate parent as long as you let go of that and give it to God! I am proud to say that I am a desperate parent, and that God is my pilot as I navigate this journey.

Thanks Kia, for listening to God and sharing the encouragement Jesus gives to help desperate parents realize that there is hope!

Stephen "Doc" Hunsley, M.D.
SOAR Special Needs
Executive Director/Founder
Overland Park, Kansas
SOARspecialneeds.org
doc@soarspecialneeds.org

> I have found that in order to heal—physically and emotionally—I need to serve.

Introduction

I've been trying to break a bad habit. God will suggest I do something, and I'll dismiss it as a notion from my silly mind. But God will nudge me again, maybe through the words of a friend or something that pops up on social media. I'll think, maybe that is a God-idea, but I'm sure someone else has it covered.

Another "coincidence" or few will catch my attention and I might acknowledge that the banging sound I hear is the Lord knocking on my thick skull. I may even get motivated for a moment before deciding I'm too busy. Then, I'll find myself up early on a Saturday morning—knowing no one else will be awake for hours—and I'll feel God saying, now would be a good time to do that thing I've been asking you to do. And I'll say, God, I don't have the brain-power for that right now. Binge-watching Netflix is more my speed.

Eventually God's tugging me toward his plan is the first thing I think of when I wake up and the last thing that crosses my mind as I go to sleep. And when I finally quit stalling it is so rewarding that I wonder what took me so long. I wonder why God kept calling me.

This book was born of such a process. And while it should not have taken me years to write, God didn't nag or make me feel guilty about my reluctance. He was simply, lovingly patient. I still need to break some bad habits, but I think the timing was his plan all along. Because that kind of patient love is part of what he wanted to teach me about raising my son.

Which brings us to desperate parenting.

What does it take to claim the dubious title of desperate parent? The details may look different for each of us but we have this in common: We're in over our heads with this parenting thing. And we know it.

> When you turn to God in desperation it doesn't mean you never prayed for help before. It means this time you don't have a backup plan.

Since you're reading this book, perhaps the word desperate resonates with you. Or maybe you aren't quite desperate yet, but it looks like the next stop on a train that's moving a little too fast. If we were sitting together over coffee I'd ask your story. What is making you feel desperate?

For me it was a son struggling with ADHD, anxiety and defiance. For Brandon and Pam it was the stress of protecting a son with autism. For Carrie it was seeing her daughter suffer through a relentless barrage of illnesses. For John it was the isolation of depression. For Kirsten it was the heartache of a son with an addiction. What about you?

Think about that for a few minutes. Identify where you have been, where you are, and where you hope to be. I started out optimistic and determined to find a solution to "fix" our son. At some point that changed to feeling like a failure as a mother. Eventually I cried out to Jesus, "How would you raise him? Because I can't."

So, I gave up.

Let me be clear about what I was giving up. I did not give up loving and working hard for my child. I did not back off every opportunity I could grasp for him. I let go of what I could never accomplish in the first place. I gave up trying to be his savior.

When you turn to God in desperation it doesn't mean you never prayed for help before. It means this time you don't have a back-up plan. There is no choice but to be honest with God and say, "My love is not enough to fix my child's struggles."

But God is enough. I'm not saying he will fix all your problems. I'm saying, he is always there for you. Would you like to know a secret? Reaching the end of your rope can be a good thing. Really. It gives you no choice but to look outside yourself for help. How can God catch you unless you let go of the rope? And the sooner you release your grip the fewer rope burns you'll have.

I feel your doubt. This was a difficult step for me. I would rather cling with bloody hands to the end of my rope than give up control. Here's the lovely thing about God: It doesn't matter if it took me too long to let go. He doesn't care that I turned to him as a last resort. He's just glad I asked for help. Because now we can make some progress.

Like me, you probably just want to do what's best for your child. But when my best wasn't enough I turned to Jesus (with less-than-reverent frustration) and asked for help. He answered. He prompted me to open my Bible and find what he said to the other parents who came to him in desperation. How simple is that? And as it turns out, profoundly applicable.

> How can God catch you unless you let go of the rope?

This book is not about comparing circumstances. There will always be someone with more difficult challenges than your own. But reaching a point of desperation is real for each of us. We are each looking for our turning points, and learning how to move forward in a better direction—with God leading our steps.

Successfully parenting kids is an ever-moving target. What works well for one family, may not work for another. What worked well for a while may not work anymore. That is why advice is a tricky thing. Whether it's from a well-meaning neighbor or a PhD who has sold a million books, you never know where you're going to find the gems or the junk. I would not presume to offer you my parenting advice. The only advice I'm really interested in sharing with you is what I have learned from Jesus.

Throughout this book, all of Jesus's words are in **_bold italic_** so you can distinguish **_Jesus's_** voice. He's giving us the only answer that is true for all of us: We should love our kids the way Jesus would. His advice should not contradict any plan or therapy you have in place for your child. What he shares with us is useful for any parent—desperate or not.

You will get more from this book if you keep this in mind: It is not about changing your child, it's about seeing him or her through different eyes. It's about changing _yourself_ to be more like Jesus. Don't let that idea overwhelm you. Give yourself some grace. After all, Jesus does, and that's exactly what he wants us to model for our kids.

One more thing before you proceed. Whether you consider yourself desperate or not, you're invited to join the **Desperate Parents Club**. Find us on Facebook to fellowship with other parents reading this book, or going through the study guide with a small group. As a virtual community we pray, encourage, and learn together. I hope to talk with you there.

> Throughout this book, all of Jesus's words are in **_bold italic_** so you can distinguish **Jesus's** voice.

Chapter 1

Jesus, How Would You Raise My Kid?

Is there a single event that marks the moment you realized you have zero control? Or is it more like an endless line of incidents that blur into helplessness? For me it was the former—at a hotel in Memphis.

We were driving home from a family vacation—a 4-day cruise with a two-day drive on either side. My mind wandered over the previous week as the miles passed. It had been a while since I'd spent that much uninterrupted time with my eight-year-old son Caden, and I was taking stock. The trip had created those fun, family memories we were hoping for, but there were definitely low moments. We had the usual arguments, a couple of meltdowns, a disciplinary meeting with a camp counselor, and constant stress that his daredevil antics would land him in the sea.

We already knew Caden had behavior issues. We had been systematically addressing our concerns for a couple years, trying and rejecting one approach after another. The past week put the results on display. Bottomline: A lot of work had produced minimal results. But I still felt we had things under control. There were still methods left to try and I am a determined person who likes to have a plan. Read that as, I like to be in control.

We stopped for the night at a hotel in Memphis. The next morning Caden woke up in a bad mood and it went downhill from there. We went to breakfast in the lobby. He argued about everything, complained loudly, and disrupted the entire breakfast area. My husband and our older son Ethan left to gather our luggage so we could check out. I stayed with Caden to finish breakfast.

I don't remember exactly what lit the fuse, but the bomb exploded. He yelled that he was going to kill himself by running into traffic. He jumped up from the table and started toward the exit.

In the half-second I had to assess the situation I decided there was a 50/50 chance he would actually do it. I couldn't risk calling his bluff. I ran after him and grabbed him. He struggled against me with more strength than I would have thought possible for an eight-year-old. We fell to the floor and I latched my arms and legs around him. He continued to buck, bite, scratch, and cry. By this time I was crying too.

A few minutes later my husband came back to the lobby and disentangled us. Somehow we made it to the car and started home. But I was changed. My confidence was shattered. This was way beyond my ability to handle. I looked helplessly at my husband and he returned my look. I realized he'd reached the same conclusion—probably sooner.

Now What?

What do you do after admitting you can't help your own child? I love him, but I don't have the power to help him. Yes, we talked to doctors and counselors. And for the first time we genuinely turned to God. Of course we'd been praying for Caden all along, but truthfully we were still leaning on our own solutions. This may sound like a weird thing for someone who has been a

Christian most of her life to say, but I realized I didn't know how fully trusting God was supposed to work. How do you tell God you're not sure how to rely on him?

As we searched for solutions to Caden's behavior issues and anxieties we tried tips and tricks from doctors, teachers, and counselors. We tried a series of diet modifications. We tried good, old-fashioned firmness and consequence. We had stacks of books to read. We attended parenting classes and seminars. And we prayed through all of that. But if I'm honest, I may have been putting more hope in the next thing on our list to try than I was on God—until we ran out of things to try.

I'm not saying all of our previous efforts were useless. In hindsight I can see how God used even the times we didn't listen to him to teach us. Those lessons brought us closer to him. Those failures highlighted the difference between me being in control and God being in control. I needed to reach a place of utter desperation to say, "Jesus, how would you raise my kid?"

> How do you tell God you're not sure how to rely on him?

I asked and he answered. I just didn't hear what he was trying to tell me—at first. I was too busy looking for books, websites, and support groups that might answer my question. Jesus kept whispering that I just needed to pick up my Bible.

Amazingly, the conviction didn't diminish. In fact, his direction grew more urgent and specific. The essence of what he was telling me to do was so simple, I ran out of excuses. It was simply this: Find and read all the interactions Jesus had with parents in the Bible.

So I did. I found it stunningly appropriate to my situation. I started keeping notes and journaling. My Bible has all of Jesus' words in red. The red letters began to feel like food to me. I hungrily continued through the New Testament looking for red. I read each word Jesus spoke, asking if he could be speaking to me.

Of course, not everything Jesus said had special meaning for me personally. I'll take a pass on what he had to say to the Pharisees. Harsh! But from conviction to encouragement there were far more soul-touching messages than I would have dreamed. I felt like he was talking directly to me. Try it. He's talking to you too.

Start Here.

In Matthew 11:28-30 Jesus said, *"Come to Me, all you who labor and are heavy laden, and I will give you rest. Take my yoke upon you and learn from me, for I am gentle and lowly in heart, and you will find rest for your souls. For my yoke is easy and my burden is light."* (NKJV)

Even as I read these words for the umpteenth time I am still blown away. Jesus starts by saying he understands my desperation. He doesn't berate me for all the ways I've messed up. Picture that verse in your mind. A yoke is a big wooden device that goes across the necks of two oxen. It is hooked to a plow or cart so they can walk side-by-side combining their strength to pull the load. What is unexpected is that Jesus does not position himself as the farmer in the cart cracking the whip. He puts himself in the yoke by my side, sharing the work *with* me. More than that, he promises the burden will be light. He is saying he'll bear the brunt of the load as I learn his ways.

Few things are stronger than a parent's love. Yet somehow, that's not enough. For our family, it hasn't been enough to stop the countless meetings with teachers and principals. It was not enough to repair damaged relationships with peers or their parents. My love for my son couldn't force coaches to give him another chance. It couldn't convince him to stop and think before doing or saying something he'd regret. No amount of my love can control any of these things. That's why this is not about changing my child. It's about changing myself. And that, I think, will be challenging enough.

After His resurrection, on one of his last days physically on this earth, Jesus had a conversation with Simon Peter. *"Do you love me?"* he asked. Peter replied that he did. *"Feed my lambs."* Jesus said. Then he asked a second time, *"Do you love me?"* Peter answered, *"Yes, Lord; You know that I love you."* Jesus said, *"Tend my sheep."* Then he said a third time, *"Simon, do you love me?"* Peter, likely distressed that Jesus needed to ask three times, assured him that he loved him. Jesus told him, *"Feed my sheep."* (John 21:12-17, NKJV)

Why do you think Jesus repeated the request three times? Perhaps Peter needed to remember the three times he denied knowing Jesus, (Luke 22:54-62) but I think there is a more important reason. Jesus doesn't dwell on our mistakes, he points us toward his plans for our future. Jesus knew Peter's future. Peter would become an instrumental leader as Christianity began to grow and spread. I think Jesus knew that teaching, caring for, and loving people is not always easy, and he wanted Peter to fully understand the commitment he was making.

Our human love can be weak. There will be times when we're beaten down, angry, frustrated, and our human capacity to love will fail us. A commitment helps. Jesus asked Peter to make a covenant and repeat it three times to burn it on his heart. Jesus went further. He finished this conversation with Peter by telling him exactly how to keep his promise saying, *"Follow me."* (John 21:19, NKJV)

> Our human love can be weak. There will be times when we're beaten down, angry, frustrated, and our human capacity to love will fail us.

So here we are, like Peter, at the start. Your commitment to your child may be obvious in your mind, but let's put it into words. Jesus is asking you, *"Do you love me?"* He is challenging you to, *"Feed my lambs."* Stop now and answer him. Make the promise you need to make. You might even write your own personal covenant and accept the weight of it. Tell Him, "Lord, I love you and I promise to care for this child you have entrusted to me." Put it into words that mean something specific to you. Acknowledge that these are not words to be spoken lightly. Say them as you wake and as you fall asleep. Use them as your mantra to refocus your spirit in difficult moments. Remember the commitment you've made and then relax into Jesus's next step, *"Follow me."*

With those words, we are to become students of Christ, emulating him as much as we can. Not only do we have the Word of God, documenting so much of Jesus's sayings and doings here on earth, he also directs us to the Holy Spirit who will live in and through us—now and always. (John 14:16-17 and 26) We have constant access to his truth, power, correction, and comfort. This is really good news. I need all the help I can get. Like Peter, I need reminders, do-overs, mercy.

God loves a repentant heart, he also needs us to sincerely seek to follow the path he provided. When we have a child (or children), our call to be like Jesus is incredibly important. And if you have a child (or children) with struggles, your demonstration of Jesus is critical.

No pressure, right? Let's keep it in perspective. As much as you need mercy, understanding, acceptance, and love—so does your child. We're giving what we would ask for ourselves. But Jesus does it so much better, so we ask for his help.

Chapter 2

Desperate Parents Club, First Century Edition

Obviously, you and I are not the founding members of the desperate parents club. Countless parents have hit the wall of realization that they can't fix their child's problems. It takes some of us a long time of beating our heads against that wall before we look to Jesus for help. There was a point where I had to say, "Lord, I am failing this child you gave me. You're going to have to step in." I imagine him replying, "I'm so glad you asked. Now we can get to work." That was a turning point for me; the first steps down a better road—albeit with detours where I try to resume control. I'm still navigating the path, but learning how to let God lead.

In the Bible, an interesting assortment of parents came to Jesus after reaching the end of their rope. Realizing that their love was not enough to save their children, they put pride, fear, and doubt aside and found faith.

In this chapter we will read the stories of four such people. First, you will find the account of each first century desperate parent directly from the Bible. Then, as a way to better understand these stories from the parent's point of view I share a fictional version of each.

Do you ever read something in the Bible and have about a dozen questions? I want more details. I need some backstory. I'd like to ask those parents what they were feeling and what it was like to look into Jesus's eyes? Using the scant details in the Bible and a little bit of research about first century life, I imagined what each mom or dad might have experienced.

After reading the Bible's account I hope you'll enjoy reading how I envision each story. These events may have happened thousands of years ago but I think you'll be able to relate. This is what I'd like you to remember as we proceed: We are studying these stories, not to compare the specific needs of those children with our own, but to identify with other parents who gave up trying to fix their problems and turned to the Lord for help.

Jairus
Luke 8:41-56 (NKJV) Also see Matthew 9:18-26 and Mark 5:22-43.

41 And behold, there came a man named Jairus, and he was a ruler of the synagogue. And he fell down at Jesus's feet and begged Him to come to his house, 42 for he had an only daughter about twelve years of age, and she was dying.

But as He went, the multitudes thronged Him. 43 Now a woman, having a flow of blood for twelve years, who had spent all her livelihood on physicians and could not be healed by any, 44 came from behind and touched the border of His garment. And immediately her flow of blood stopped.

45 And Jesus said, "Who touched Me?"

When all denied it, Peter and those with him said, "Master, the multitudes throng and press You, and You say, 'Who touched Me?' "

46 But Jesus said, "Somebody touched Me, for I perceived power going out from Me." 47 Now when the woman saw that she was not hidden, she came trembling; and falling down before Him, she declared to Him in the presence of all the people the reason she had touched Him and how she was healed immediately.

48 And He said to her, "Daughter, be of good cheer; your faith has made you well. Go in peace."

49 While He was still speaking, someone came from the ruler of the synagogue's house, saying to him, "Your daughter is dead. Do not trouble the Teacher."

50 But when Jesus heard it, He answered him, saying, "Do not be afraid; only believe, and she will be made well." 51 When He came into the house, He permitted no one to go in except Peter, James, and John, and the father and mother of the girl. 52 Now all wept and mourned for her; but He said, "Do not weep; she is not dead, but sleeping." 53 And they ridiculed Him, knowing that she was dead.

54 But He put them all outside, took her by the hand and called, saying, "Little girl, arise." 55 Then her spirit returned, and she arose immediately. And He commanded that she be given something to eat. 56 And her parents were astonished, but He charged them to tell no one what had happened.

"Do not be afraid; only believe."

How I Imagine Jairus's Story

"There is nothing else I can do. I'm sorry." Jairus felt the weight of the physician's hand on his shoulder as he left the room—a transfer of burden from doctor to father. Sinking to the floor by his daughter's bed, he touched her cool, sunken cheek. The contrast of his sun-darkened hand against her pale skin startled him. He snached his hand away. Instead, he pulled the blanket up under her chin and tucked the edges around her frail body. If he didn't know she was 12 years old he would have guessed years younger.

Whether she was sleeping or unconscious was hard to tell, but her chest rose and fell slightly with barely audible breaths. He clamped his eyes shut and willed her to breathe deeply and clearly. He tried to pray, but there was no new prayer to recite. All he could manage was vague begging aimed in God's direction. The only response was her wheezy breathing. Each faint rattle echoed in his head, judging his failure as a father.

There had to be something else he could *do*.

The rabbi had prayed for her. Doctors had assessed her. He and his wife had followed every instruction for her care. He was the leader of the synagogue for heaven's sake. The whole community knew of Talitha's illness. Today, dozens of people invaded his home—and his mind—with their sympathetic chattering. Why were they here? All at once they reminded him of vultures circling, waiting for prey to die. Revolting. He wished they would go away.

He wrestled yet again with the Jesus option. Jairus wasn't sure he believed the reports about the healing teacher, but oh, he wanted to right now. He pushed the thought aside. He could lose his job. Jesus was not on his superiors' approval list. Their threats against anyone who followed or spoke well of Jesus made that clear.

Maintaining the synagogue and arranging the services gave him purpose, made him feel closer to God. He liked his job. He had worked hard to earn the appointment. But he loved his daughter, his only child. Would it make God angry if he talked to Jesus? A low moan escaped Talatha's throat. Jairus covered his face with his hand and moaned too—if only to mask the sound of her suffering.

The name Jesus became a pulse in his mind. He had to try. There was no time left, no pride left, and only enough hope left to propel him to his feet and out the door. He quizzed a few people to see where he could find Jesus, then sprinted off to the shore. Sure enough, a large crowd choked an area of the beach. Undeterred, he pushed his way through until, abruptly, he was face to face with the teacher.

Jesus looked at him expectantly. Jairus fell at Jesus's feet. For a moment even the crowd was silent. Then he dared to look up, found his courage and said, *"My little daughter is at the point of death. Come and lay your hands on her, so that she may be made well and live."* Jesus said nothing, but nodded and strode away as the crowd parted. Jairus scrambled up from the dirt and followed.

Jesus seemed to know the way without directions. They moved quickly despite the jostling of the crowd swarming around them. Still, Jairus's chest throbbed with impatience to reach his daughter.

Then, Jesus simply stopped. *"Who touched me?"* He said.

With the abrupt halt the mass of the crowd caught up and surrounded them creating a small stage for the action. Jesus turned in a slow circle, making eye contact with those closest to him. Jairus clenched his jaw in frustration. One of his disciples replied by stating the obvious. *"Master, people are all around you, pushing against you."*

Jairus was on the verge of physically yanking Jesus toward his home when a trembling woman approached and knelt. She explained that she had spent all her money hoping to cure a discharge of blood that had troubled her for 12 years. The crowd took a visible step back. Jairus's mouth twisted in disgust. If she was bleeding she was unclean.

She continued, *"I was thinking, if I can just touch his clothes I will be healed."* Jairus eyed the hem of Jesus's robe. Could it be that easy? What if he ... But Jesus interrupted his thought and said to the woman, *"Daughter, your faith has healed you. Go in peace and be freed from your suffering."* There was nothing special about Jesus's clothes. Her faith and the power of Jesus freed her from 12 years of isolation. 12 years—the same age as his daughter. There had to be hope for Talitha too.

Hope, however, was crushed by the arrival of messengers from Jairus's house. *"Your daughter is dead. There is no need to bother the teacher?"* Jairus couldn't find his next breath. The ground seemed to shift under his feet. Jesus steadied him, looked into his eyes and spoke directly to him for the first time. *"Do not fear, only believe."* Then he resumed his brisk pace toward Jairus's house.

Before he could see them Jairus heard the human vultures. Wails and mourning cries assaulted his ears and his faith. His daughter was dead, truly. Jesus walked up to the loudest of the mourners and said, *"Why all this commotion and wailing? The child is not dead but asleep."* Laughter replaced their wailing. Jairus was momentarily fascinated by the mourners' quick transition from theatrical sorrow to cruel amusement. The truth of their presence snapped into focus. Attention was their feast, gossip their dessert.

With unchallenged authority Jesus cleared the house. He gathered only three of his followers and asked Jairus and his wife to lead the way. The six of them crowded into the girl's room and surrounded her bed.

Jairus stared at the still, pale figure on the bed. He heard the stifled sobs of his wife and pulled her close. Leaning in he whispered, "Jesus said she is only sleeping." He closed his eyes and pictured his daughter asleep. Dark lashes rested on plump, pink cheeks. Her chest rose and fell in natural rhythm. Was there anything more beautiful?

He opened his eyes to see Jesus approach the bed. He took her hand and said, *"Child, arise."* Miraculously she did exactly that. She stood next to Jesus with her bed clothes hanging from emaciated shoulders. Jairus heard his wife gasp. His vision blurred with tears and he felt his wife pull away moving toward their child.

Jairus, however, covered his face with his hands. His shoulders clenched under the weight of the guilt and fear he had been carrying. Why did he wait so long to find Jesus? He felt a hand squeeze his shoulder. He raised his head and looked into Jesus's eyes. He must have expected judgment from the teacher because the love he saw instead caught him by surprise. Once again a hand on his shoulder signified a transfer of burden. This time heaviness lifted, and peace moved up through his body like it might raise his feet off the floor.

Jesus guided him to join his wife and daughter's celebration in progress. Before he left he gave them two instructions: Give her something to eat, and tell no one what had happened. The first oddly obvious and the second oddly impossible. They would just have to stick to the truth. She was only sleeping.

"Child, arise"

The Syrophenician Woman

Mark 7:24-30 (NKJV) Also see Matthew 15:21-28.

24 From there He arose and went to the region of Tyre and Sidon. And He entered a house and wanted no one to know it, but He could not be hidden. 25 For a woman whose young daughter had an unclean spirit heard about Him, and she came and fell at His feet. 26 The woman was a Greek, a Syro-Phoenician by birth, and she kept asking Him to cast the demon out of her daughter. 27 But Jesus said to her, "Let the children be filled first, for it is not good to take the children's bread and throw it to the little dogs."

28 And she answered and said to Him, "Yes, Lord, yet even the little dogs under the table eat from the children's crumbs."

29 Then He said to her, "For this saying go your way; the demon has gone out of your daughter."

30 And when she had come to her house, she found the demon gone out, and her daughter lying on the bed.

How I Imagine The Syrophenician Woman's Story

From the corner of the one-room house she inventoried the damage. She could glimpse a bit of blue sky through a small, round hole in the wall. The size of the hole was a clear match to the broom handle on the floor below the puncture. Splinters protruded from the broken shaft. It occurred to her that it was now the right height for a three-year-old child to use. She counted two unstuffed cushions, a broken pitcher, and a shattered cup—their last one.

The eastern window cast a rectangle of light in the center of the room. Its bright boundaries framed a nightgown crumpled on the floor. Crescents of red patterned the otherwise colorless cloth—the unmistakable shape of a human bite.

A tingling sensation drew her attention to her forearm. Two crescents formed an oval in her flesh. At first she couldn't make sense of the shape, but as the meaning penetrated the fog of her mind the tingle began to throb. She ignored it, hoping to recapture the cloudiness of disbelief. But it was too late. Reality prevailed.

Her gaze shifted to the now peaceful face of her young daughter. She lifted a hand to stroke the hair fanned out over her lap, then thought better of any movement that might wake her. Love and terror pulled at either side of her chest. She wondered which was stronger and if she would survive the war.

How was it possible? This child, only as tall as her waist, had ravaged their house like a keleb—a wild and savage dog. She cringed at the comparison, but conceded it was appropriate. The word itself was a curse, an insult. In the throes of an episode, her daughter's strength was inhuman, her fury demonic. And there it was, the diagnosis sentenced upon them by doctors and priests: possessed by a demon. She could not refute it. What else could explain the hell they lived in?

It must be her fault, her sin, that brought this on them. That was what her husband said when he threw them out and barred the doors. She had to agree. Her little girl could not have invited this. She honored and sacrificed to as many gods as she could, begging for the removal of the curse. But there were so many gods. Apparently she had offended one of them irreparably.

Her brother conditionally agreed to take her and her daughter in. As a trade merchant with a fleet of ships, his estate was on the coast near the bustling port of Tyre. They were put in a small sea shack where the crash of waves and wail of winds masked the shrieks of a raving girl. From there she lived as a sort of servant, mending, cleaning, and whatever else was asked of her.

Which reminded her, she had work to do. She eased out from under her daughter's head as gently as she could. Ignoring the chaos in the room, she walked to the door, opened it and stepped into the light. Even before her eyes adjusted enough to see the flattened ears and raised spine, she heard a warning growl from the dog crouched in front of her.

"Kynarion!" She said with more authority than she felt. She had acquired the dog as a puppy from local shepherds, raising him to protect their house. She still called him kynarion, the word for puppy, though he now weighed as much as she did. He could kill her if he had a mind to. Fortunately he preferred the rats and reptiles around their house. He usually slept right outside their door. He never came inside unless she invited him to clean up scraps off the floor around their table. But when the demons came the dog wouldn't come near the house. He growled and barked from a safe radius.

Relaxing his attack stance the dog sniffed the air and ventured near his master. She rewarded him with a scratch behind one ear, then turned to her work. Releasing the dried laundry from its lines she carefully folded and bundled it into a large sheet which she cinched at the top and slung on her back. With a "stay" command to Kynarion, she trudged toward the main house.

17

The cook was the first to share the news—along with a shopping list for her to fill. By the time she had retrieved half of the list she'd heard four different versions of the same story. This last telling was from the baker. Owing to the fact that he had provided a large delivery of baked goods to the house in question, she gave the gossip her full attention

According to the rumor a healing rabbi named Jesus from Israel was staying in their town. Right here. Right now! She had considered taking her daughter to him in the past. But traveling with her daughter was both unwise and unaffordable. She never expected him to show up here. Her mind started racing. A spark of hope ignited in her soul. She dropped her bag, mumbled that she'd be back to get it later, and turned to leave.

"Wait," the baker said. "The Israelites are trying to keep their presence quiet. You won't be welcomed there." She shrugged and kept going. Welcomed? She wasn't welcome anywhere. Even a tiny chance of healing for her daughter was worth any risk.

At the intersection of two roads she hesitated. Go back the miles to her house to get her daughter or go the short distance to the house where Jesus was staying? Stay close, her instinct told her. And yet she stood there, paralyzed by doubt. How could she possibly approach him? She was a woman. She was an outcast. And most significantly, she was a gentile. He was a Jew. She didn't even know how to worship his God.

A figure passed briskly in front of her with a young girl trailing by several paces. The child picked a roadside wildflower, then ran to catch up with her mother. Another bloom caught the girl's eye. She stopped to add it to her growing bouquet, then darted ahead to grasp her mother's robe. She watched the little routine replay until the pair turned into their house.

Something clarified in her heart and resolution released her from doubt. She would find Jesus and ask for his help. She would not take no for an answer. Turning right, she walked purposefully up the road. Before going more than a dozen steps she saw a crowd filling the road and coming toward her. She moved to the side.

Already anticipating that this could be the Israelites she sought, she examined them as they approached. The group of men talked amongst themselves as they walked. They did not acknowledge her, or even seem to see her, but somehow their mass reformed to avoid coming close to her. They were a single-minded, impenetrable bubble—all but one man toward the front. He was unremarkable in any way except one. He looked at her.

His eyes stayed with her until the group had nearly passed. Then she found her voice and yelled out, *"Lord, Son of David, have mercy on me! My daughter is demon-possessed and suffering terribly."* Even to her own ears, her voice sounded shrill and annoying.

They ignored her—in an intentional way. She followed, repeating her cry with growing volume. The one she assumed was Jesus appeared oblivious. The others finally looked at her, but only long enough to glare. Passers-by were starting to notice, some of them turning to follow the parade.

She heard one of the men say to the man who, indeed, must be their leader, *"Send her away, for she keeps crying out after us."* What did that mean? Was he suggesting Jesus grant her request just to quiet her? She ran to the front of the group and stood in their path and raised her request again.

Jesus stopped before her. He did not speak to her, but replied to the disciple who had spoken, *"I was sent only to the lost sheep of Israel."* Then he moved to one side and resumed his pace. The rest of the group followed, leaving a wide area around her.

Undeterred, she raced ahead of them again. She threw herself on the ground, humbling herself for the sake of her daughter. Again, he stopped in front of her. She dared to look up, and in hardly more than a whisper she said, *"Lord, help me."* This time he spoke to her, ***"Let the children be fed first, for it is not fair to take the children's food and throw it to the dogs."***

She winced at the insult but held his gaze. Was that a hint of a smile at the corner of his mouth? Was he laughing at her or was it something more? She played back his words in her mind. Two things stood out. He used the word kynarion for dog, rather than the more insulting keleb. And he said *first,* the children of Israel would be fed first. That meant there would be a second course for the gentiles!

Jesus's smile grew, encouraging her to speak. She said, *"Sir, even the dogs under the table eat the children's crumbs."* He laughed loudly and looked at his disciples to make sure they got the joke. Turning back to her, he said, ***"Woman, you have great faith! Your request is granted."***

She knew. Even before she thanked him, scrambled to her feet and ran away, she knew what she would find at home. She could see it in her mind as clearly as truth. Her daughter would be sitting on the bed, wrapped in a blanket. The child's eyes would be clear and peaceful, with her arms outstretched to welcome her mother's love. And Kynarian would be resting in front of their house, ready to protect them from the outside, never again on guard against the demons within.

> *"Woman, you have great faith!"*

The Royal Official
John 4:46-53 (NKJV)

46 So Jesus came again to Cana of Galilee where He had made the water wine. And there was a certain nobleman whose son was sick at Capernaum. 47 When he heard that Jesus had come out of Judea into Galilee, he went to Him and implored Him to come down and heal his son, for he was at the point of death. 48 Then Jesus said to him, "Unless you people see signs and wonders, you will by no means believe."

49 The nobleman said to Him, "Sir, come down before my child dies!"

50 Jesus said to him, "Go your way; your son lives." So the man believed the word that Jesus spoke to him, and he went his way. 51 And as he was now going down, his servants met him and told him, saying, "Your son lives!"

52 Then he inquired of them the hour when he got better. And they said to him, "Yesterday at the seventh hour the fever left him." 53 So the father knew that it was at the same hour in which Jesus said to him, "Your son lives." And he himself believed, and his whole household.

"Go your way ... "

How I imagine The Royal Official's Story

His aimless pacing wouldn't make the night any shorter. And yet he paced. Stopping at the front door he jerked it open and strained to see past the pool of light cast by the lamp in his outstretched hand. Nothing. No one. The darkness offered no sign of dawn. He started to slam the door but caught it before it crashed shut. There was no point alarming the rest of the house.

He walked down the hall to his son's room. He confirmed the familiar view through the half-opened door. Even outside the room the bitter smell of healing herbs made his nose twitch. Water splashed as a servant dipped a cloth, wrung it out and applied it to his son's brow. The wet sound complimented the tears streaming down his wife's face as she sat in vigil beside the bed.

A timid knock at the front door pulled him away from the scene. If someone was worried he was sleeping, they needn't. He couldn't. Racing to the door he opened it to see a hand raised to knock again. He asked, "Did you find him?" The messenger bowed respectfully, nodded and said, "Cana."

Only twenty miles away was a man named Jesus who might be able to heal his son. Now he had a mission. Without another thought he grabbed his coat, the lamp, and strode into the darkness.

An hour later he yelped as his toe made contact with yet another rock camouflaged by the pre-dawn gloom. The lamp had gone out but he stumbled ahead, willing the sun to rise. Twenty miles no longer seemed a minor distance. He paused to rub his calves and glare back down the hill at the few miles he had conquered. Then, as the sun's first rays broke over the horizon, his outlook brightened. He would get to Cana, find Jesus, and bring him back to his home. By this evening his boy could be well. He picked up his pace.

Ten miles later he cursed the sun as sweat trickled down his back. He fashioned his belt into a makeshift turban and abandoned his coat. Why did he walk? If he had waited for daylight he could have arranged for a horse. The growling from his gut reminded him that he brought no food or money. What was he thinking? And why would Jesus agree to walk twenty miles back to his home tonight? Pushing the negativity aside he focused on success. He was a nobleman, an official in King Herod's service. He always found a way to get things done. Failure was not an option. Jesus would simply have to come.

The royal official arrived in Cana as the sun reached its height. The long walk had hardened his resolve. His first stop was to the leader of the town to get some intelligence. Yes, Jesus was in town—somewhere. Try the synagogue. Pausing only for a drink of water the official rushed to the synagogue. From there he was directed to a series of other locations without success. A growing crowd trailed behind him as the word spread: Someone important was going to ask Jesus for a miracle.

After an hour of racing around Cana the official finally found his target. He walked up to Jesus with confidence, feeling he had earned something for his effort. Even so, he bowed his head and respectfully implored Jesus. *"Sir, please come with me to my house. My son is near death. Please, will you heal him?"* Jesus looked around at the crowd gathered, then looked at the official and said to him, *"Unless you people see signs and wonders, you will by no means believe."*

He looked at Jesus blankly, not sure what he meant. Undeterred from his mission, he repeated his request with urgency. *"Sir, come down before my child dies!"* Jesus looked at him for a long, meaningful moment and said, *"Go your way; your son lives."* A sequence of surprise, shame, and hope struck the official. Jesus had not agreed to come to his house as he expected, no, demanded. Instead, he stripped away his entitlement—but also offered him a lifeline. Silence hung in the air as he processed Jesus's words: *unless you see you won't believe.* Could he believe without seeing? Maybe. This man seemed to see into his soul. Surely his power could reach twenty miles to heal his son.

He decided. With nothing more than a nod to Jesus the royal official believed, turned, and began his long walk home. The crowd dispersed, grumbling.

Hours down the road, the setting sun lengthened the man-shaped shadow in front of him. The shape blurred and he stumbled. An involuntary grimace cracked his lip, filling his mouth with the metallic taste of blood. He forced himself to take another step. And another. He longed to get home, but his body rebelled. He leaned against a tree, then slumped to the ground. He mumbled, "I believe," and closed his eyes.

Morning light woke him. He staggered to his feet and resumed his journey. He was heading east into the rising sun, so he didn't see the approaching figures until they were right in front of him. His servants surrounded him and gave him the news. *"Your son lives!"* Those words were familiar. "What time?" He asked his servants. "When exactly did my son recover?" They said, *"Yesterday, at one in the afternoon, the fever left him."* He stared at them, speechless. At exactly that time Jesus had said, *"Go your way; your son lives."*

He said he believed, but he only believed that Jesus could heal his son. Now he believed that Jesus was more than just a man. He was holy. He was quite possibly the Messiah, the Son of God. Jesus was a King worth serving.

Revived by joy he completed the journey home with surprising speed. The front door flew open before he reached it. His son—

flush with health instead of fever—ran into his arms. Without letting go of his child he found his wife, then gathered their servants. He told them everything that happened. And they all believed.

The Man with the Epileptic Son

Mark 9:14-27 (NKJV) Also see Matthew 17:14-21 and Luke 9:37-42.

14 And when He came to the disciples, He saw a great multitude around them, and scribes disputing with them. 15 Immediately, when they saw Him, all the people were greatly amazed, and running to Him, greeted Him. 16 And He asked the scribes, "What are you discussing with them?"

17 Then one of the crowd answered and said, "Teacher, I brought You my son, who has a mute spirit. 18 And wherever it seizes him, it throws him down; he foams at the mouth, gnashes his teeth, and becomes rigid. So I spoke to Your disciples, that they should cast it out, but they could not."

19 He answered him and said, "O faithless generation, how long shall I be with you? How long shall I bear with you? Bring him to Me." 20 Then they brought him to Him. And when he saw Him, immediately the spirit convulsed him, and he fell on the ground and wallowed, foaming at the mouth.

21 So He asked his father, "How long has this been happening to him?"

And he said, "From childhood. 22 And often he has thrown him both into the fire and into the water to destroy him. But if You can do anything, have compassion on us and help us."

23 Jesus said to him, "If you can believe, all things are possible to him who believes."

24 Immediately the father of the child cried out and said with tears, "Lord, I believe; help my unbelief!"

25 When Jesus saw that the people came running together, He rebuked the unclean spirit, saying to it, "Deaf and dumb spirit, I command you, come out of him and enter him no more!" 26 Then the spirit cried out, convulsed him greatly, and came out of him. And he became as one dead, so that many said, "He is dead." 27 But Jesus took him by the hand and lifted him up, and he arose.

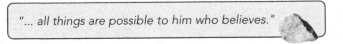

"... all things are possible to him who believes."

How I Imagine The Man with the Epileptic Son's Story

Chaos surrounded him. On his right, a group of Jesus's disciples shouted arguments and shook their fists. On his left, several scribes wagged fingers, and shouted louder. A growing crowd of gawkers pressed in, choosing sides and voicing their opinions. He retreated into his mind, replaying the events that brought him here.

This mess was his fault. It started this morning when he went looking for Jesus. No wait ... his troubles started about a decade ago—when his wife died giving birth to their only child, a son. As an only son himself, and the fourth generation to carry on his family's pottery business, he looked forward to the day he could start training his son to master the clay.

That dream faltered when his son was a toddler. The child started having seizures and lost his ability to speak. He consulted his rabbi. The rabbi prayed over the child and recommended a pilgrimage to Jerusalem to offer proper sacrifices. With hopes high he made the trip with his boy and earnestly presented his gifts at the temple. But when the boy failed to improve, the rabbi declared the child was demon-possessed and banned them from the synagogue.

The verdict was a blow to his faith—and his business. Who wanted to buy pottery from a cursed family? It was a struggle but eventually the quality of his work (and his willingness to do business with the gentiles in the nearby city of Caesarea Philippi) allowed him to make a living.

He kept his boy close as he worked, but a potter's shop is a dangerous place, with sharp tools, broken pots, and a fiery kiln. As if the flames of hell were reaching out to claim his son, an attack seized him every time he was near a fire. Burn scars on his hands and face bore the evidence.

As the boy approached adolescence his size and strength made it increasingly difficult to keep him safe. "I'm doing my best," he told himself. "I can't hover over my son every moment. I must eat, sleep, and work sometimes." The hollow argument did nothing to ease his guilt. So he buried it alongside his hope and joy.

Which brought him to the present. This morning he heard that a healing rabbi was in the area. Though he had no real hope that it could change anything, neither did he have anything to lose by asking. He gathered his son and went looking for Jesus.

Instead, he found Jesus's disciples—nine of them—preaching to travelers on the road outside the village. Apparently Jesus and three of his followers had gone mountain climbing. No one knew exactly where they were or when they would be back. So he presented his son to the disciples, explained his condition, and asked them to heal him. Then he stood back with arms crossed to see what would happen.

The disciples surrounded the boy. Some of the men placed their hands on the child, others raised hands to heaven. They began to pray loudly and with confidence. They claimed his healing in the name of Jesus. They attracted an audience.

He was impressed by the forceful prayers. Maybe this could actually work. Eventually the disciples grew quiet and stepped back from his son. There was silence for a long moment. Then the boy's eyes rolled back in his head. His back arched unnaturally as he fell to the ground. His head took the impact of the fall with a sickening thud. He ran to his son and wrapped his arms around his rigid body, and wrestled the powerful spasms. After a few minutes the attack passed, leaving them in a dusty heap.

He looked at his son's face. Bluish flesh showed through a veil of dust. Foam, tinged pink with blood, bubbled out from between his clenched lips. He looked grim—like death—but he knew the boy was only unconscious with a bitten tongue. Soon his color would return and he would waken. Yes, he was embarrassed. Yes, he was anguished. He was even mildly disappointed. But those were all feelings he was used to ignoring. Today was no different than any other day, there were just more people watching.

The silence was broken by a judgemental voice. "Let that be a lesson to all of you. These Jesus-followers have no power—unless it is power from the evil one." A respected scribe from the local synagogue cast the words at the disciples like stones. Murmurs of agreement rippled through the crowd.

One of the disciples accused the scribe of standing in the way of the Lord. The scribe's face reddened. He sputtered about the audacity of hinting that Jesus was the Lord. And just like that, sides were drawn and the shouting match began. The father moved his son outside the crowd, leaned him against some large rocks, then returned to see what would happen.

The argument was intensifying when the people began to chatter and shift. A path materialized through the crowd. Looking through the space, the boy's father saw four men approaching from the mountain road. He heard someone say the name Jesus. He glanced at the disciples and saw recognition in their eyes. But they shuffled uncomfortably as they waited for their leader to approach.

The man who must be Jesus strode into the center of the crowd, scowled at his disciples, then turned to look intently at the group of scribes. Finally he looked unblinkingly at the father until he dropped his eyes to the ground. Turning back to his disciples Jesus said, *"What are you arguing about with the teachers of the law?"* No one answered so the father tried to summarize the situation. *"Teacher, I beg you to look at my son, for he is my only child. A spirit seizes him and he suddenly screams; it throws him into convulsions so that he foams at the mouth. It scarcely ever leaves him and is destroying him. I begged your disciples to drive it out, but they could not."*

That didn't really answer his question, but Jesus did not ask for clarification. Shaking his head he said, *"You people today don't believe! How long must I stay with you? How long must I be patient with you? Bring the boy to me!"* The disciples went to gather the boy. He was conscious again and walked between the men as they guided him toward their master. The child looked to his father in bewilderment. He nodded to his son with more assurance than he felt.

When they were just a few steps from Jesus, as if in reaction to his proximity, a fit seized him with unusual violence. As the boy hit the ground his father moved to his aid, but Jesus held up a hand to stop him. He obeyed and stared helplessly at his son. Jesus reclaimed the father's attention saying *"How long has this been happening to him?"*

The father looked at Jesus in surprise. No one ever asked his story. As their eyes locked the crowd seemed to blur into the background. The noise faded to a dull buzz. It was just the two of them, and Jesus's look showed genuine interest and sympathy. Though he had the impression Jesus already knew the answer, he responded. *"Since he was very young. ... If you can do anything, please have pity on us and help us."*

Jesus's eyes narrowed slightly and he said, *"Why did you say 'if you can'? All things are possible for the one who believes."* Those words struck the father's heart like a bolt of lightning. Hope surged through him with a physical force. He had been disappointed so many times he fought against hope like an enemy. But this time it felt irrepressible. He longed to embrace it.

In one impulsive burst he let down his guard and shouted, *"Lord, I believe;"* But immediately caught himself. Maybe that wasn't entirely true. He knew instinctively that there was no point being less than truthful with Jesus. So he amended his statement to a request, *"help my unbelief!"*

Jesus smiled and the jostling crowd came back into focus. Jesus turned to the boy who was still shaking on the ground and spoke in a voice that resonated off the surrounding rocks, *"You evil spirit that makes this boy deaf and stops him from talking—I command you to come out of him and never enter him again!"*

A scream came out of the boy that could not be human. His body arched as if it would break in half then shook violently for a long moment before collapsing into utter stillness. Not even breath moved his chest. Someone in the crowd voiced what he was thinking. "He is dead!" But Jesus stepped over to the boy, took hold of his hand and helped him stand up. Jesus tenderly wiped the dust and spit from his face and turned the boy toward his father. The boy spoke one of the last words he heard him say so many years ago. "Abba!" Daddy. With that word he felt the shell of his soul fill up and overflow with all the emotion he had banished.

He had come to Jesus to ask for healing for his son—not even expecting it to happen. But Jesus also healed his own dead spirit with such generosity that he had excess to share. His gratitude, joy, faith ... and so much more he could not define, was too much to keep to himself. He looked at his son with intensified love. He would pour into his son. And, he thought as he looked at the amazed faces around them, anyone else willing to listen.

> *Jesus stepped over to the boy, took hold of his hand and helped him stand up.*

How does this apply to me?

Unlike the parents in these passages, we have access to Jesus anytime, all the time. We don't need to travel any distance to talk to him about our frustrations, heartaches and fears. Believe it or not, Jesus loves your child even more than you do. His solution is to teach us, if we're willing to learn, how to love our child like he would. In the next chapter we will dig deeper into these stories examining the words of Jesus and what they mean for us here and now. Prepare yourself. He is talking to you. Please listen.

For a more in-depth study of these four stories, check out the companion to this book: *5 Tips from Jesus for Desperate Parents,*

Small Group Study Guide. The easy-to-follow workbook guides you through the Bible references in this book, offering conversation starters for your group. If you don't have a group, consider starting one. I bet you know a few other parents that would like to learn how to follow Jesus on their parenting journey. In a study group you can build friendships, share your thoughts, and learn from others. Studying the words of Jesus with others is a wonderful way to grow your faith.

We are studying these stories, not to compare the specific needs of those children with our own, but to identify with other parents who gave up trying to fix their problems and turned to the Lord for help.

Chapter 3

Five Tips from Jesus

If Jesus looked at you and said, *"Don't be afraid,"* or *"Just believe,"* do you think you could do what he asked? When he sent away the mourners or lifted a boy from the dirt, can you think of those examples as actions to follow? Looking at the interactions in the previous chapter we hear Jesus offer some repeated advice and see him do similar things. Five specific themes rise to the surface. Let's take a closer look at Jesus's words and actions, and apply them to life here and now.

Tip 1. Have Faith and Believe.

Jesus praised the Syrophoenecian woman saying, *"you have great faith!"* He challenged the father of the epileptic boy to believe. To the royal official and surrounding crowd, he accused them of believing only if they saw a miracle. In every story, Jesus mentions faith, or belief, or both. Is there a difference between faith and belief? Jesus tells us to have both, so both must be desirable. Powerful things happen with both, but perhaps there is a difference that's worth delving into. Certainly this is a topic on which whole books could be written. But for the purposes of desperate parenting consider this:

<u>Belief</u> is the unshakable confidence that a particular outcome will happen.

<u>Faith</u> is the unshakable confidence that God is good, regardless of any outcome.

Read that again, perhaps aloud. Meditate on it for a moment. What does that mean to you? Does it change anything about how you approach prayer?

Even when we are desperate most of us are still able to hope. You might call it wishing. But hopes and wishes don't really change anything. Belief is an active step toward God to trust him with your hopes.

For each of the stories there was a positive outcome for which belief was required. It's like Jesus asked the parent to picture the outcome they hoped for, then add belief that the power of God is able to produce miraculous results. When you pray with belief it is a focused prayer with a specific outcome in mind.

But what do you do when the outcome you prayed for doesn't happen?

I grew up in a Christian environment where I got the message that if you prayed hard enough and truly believed, God would provide a miracle. In my mind, if God didn't grant my request it was because my faith was weak. I'm sure I'm not alone in this. If you pray for something—like healing for a child—and it doesn't happen, you might jump to one of two conclusions: it's either my fault or God's fault.

Sometimes God doesn't answer our prayers the way we expect. This kind of disappointment can twist us into guilt, doubt or anger. This is where faith comes in. Faith simply trusts. Faith doesn't have to have proof to exist. Hebrews 11:1 says, *"Now faith is the substance of things hoped for, the evidence of things not seen."* (NKJV)

Jesus tells us to believe, and amazing things will happen. And because you *see* God's power you will be changed from the *outside-in*. Jesus also tells us to have faith. With faith amazing things will happen. But bubbling up in the *unseen* places the Holy Spirit is pouring out the gift of faith that transcends any visible outcome. And you will be changed from the *inside-out*.

This combination of belief and faith is powerful, even life-changing. That's why both are important. To believe is a verb—something you do. Romans 10:9 says, *"If you openly <u>say</u>, 'Jesus is Lord' and <u>believe</u> in your heart that God raised him from death, you will be saved."* (ERV, emphasis added) There are two actions in that verse that you can apply to your current situation; **say** it and **believe** it. Believing is where a relationship happens. We ask God for help. We talk to him about our problems, hopes and dreams. That communication creates a personal bond with God that changes our hearts.

Faith is a noun—something you have. Romans 12:3 says we are each given a measure of faith. And 1 Corinthians 12:9 says the Holy Spirit gives the gift of faith. There are also many references that our faith can be strengthened. For example, through prayer (Luke 22:32) or with the encouragement of other Christians (Romans 1:12.) This gift is a supernatural connection to God that changes our souls.

After Jesus was resurrected, he said to Thomas, the doubting disciple, *"Thomas, because you have seen Me, you have believed. Blessed are those who have not seen and yet have believed." John 20:29* (NKJV) It is understandable that Jesus was occasionally frustrated at being asked to prove himself with signs and miracles. How refreshing he must find it when we simply have faith.

> Faith simply trusts. Faith doesn't have to have proof to exist.

This simple change of perspective was revolutionary for me. Asking and believing for a miracle is a good thing that Jesus challenges us to do. Letting go of our expectations (or telling God what needs to happen) and resting in faith that God is good, is also what Jesus wants us to do. Belief gave focus and strength to my prayers. Faith released my guilt and obsession with control.

How do we get faith and belief? Follow the example of the man with the epileptic son who uttered one of the sweetest phrases in the Bible. He said, *"Help my unbelief!"* Honestly ask Jesus to provide what you lack. Whether you feel differently or not, whether you have clarity or not, have faith. Stand firm in the knowledge that God is good and wants good things for you. Believe that God will work miraculously in your family.

Perhaps the impulsive first answer that father gave Jesus was more faith-filled than it initially appeared. He spoke it. He said, *"Lord, I believe;"* because he really wanted to believe. He then asked Jesus to help him believe. And Jesus did. He'll do the same for you.

> Belief gave focus and strength to my prayers. Faith released my guilt and obsession with control.

Tip 2. Do Not Be Afraid. Do Not Weep.

Fear and negativity can be paralyzing. When bad news was brought to Jiarus and Jesus on their way to Jiarus's house, Jesus encouraged him with these words. *"Do not be afraid. Only believe."* Just as we ask for faith and belief, doubt and despair seem to raise their ugly heads.

Maybe you are fortunate enough to have friends or family who will help you remain positive, but Jiarus did not. First, messengers came to tell him his daughter was dead. Then, when they came to his house there was an unruly crowd of people mourning and wailing. Jesus told them not to weep and they ridiculed him. How did Jesus respond? He put them out of the house. Not until the negativity was kicked out—and he surrounded himself with his support team—did the miracle happen. Take note of the two steps. Jesus removed the negativity, then he created a positive and productive environment.

We watched our older son thrive in his elementary school. Caden looked forward to the day he could join his big brother, but his experience turned out to be vastly different. He was constantly in trouble, separated from classmates and activities, behind in his work, and miserable. We had been so happy with the school that it took us a few years to figure out why Caden couldn't seem to succeed there. The teachers and administration were set up to support children who fit their ideal, but not for outliers like Caden.

So we left. We couldn't afford a private school near our house so we packed up and moved to a different school district. We tried to do some research about what public district would work better for him, but ultimately it was a leap of faith. Our decision was more about removing him from a situation that had become demoralizing and negative.

> Jesus removed the negativity, then he created a positive and productive environment.

I think we would have been willing to do that again if he needed it, or homeschool him, or find a way to pay for a private school. But, praise God, the new district worked. Caden had the same struggles, but with a much more problem-solving and encouraging approach from his teachers, counselors, and principal he started succeeding. He began to enjoy school.

Think about how Jesus put the mourners out of Jiarus's house. What does that look like for you? Is the bummer in your life an environment? Is it negative people? Is it your own doubts and fears? It may not be easy, or even possible, to change some of those things.

If your environment is toxic, think about what you can do to change that situation. Hopefully it won't take an actual move, like it did for us. It may require some sacrifices, but putting your child in an encouraging setting can heal your child's emotional health.

If someone in or around your family is bringing you down, start by sharing your resolution to focus on the positive and ask everyone around you to join you. If that doesn't work, and if you can't feasibly minimize your exposure to that influence, *you* will have to be the antidote to negativity. You will have to speak encouragement to your child. You will need to shield him or her as best you can. You must stand up for them when they need an ally.

If your own heart and mind are keeping you trapped in negativity, please, reach out for help. I shed countless tears over our situation. Sometimes you need a good cry, but if that mindset is paralyzing then it's not where you need to camp out. It will seep into who you are and how you treat those around you—especially your family. The right solution for you may be a prayer partner, a support group, a therapist or counselor. All of those have been a part of my journey. I have found that when I take off my have-it-all-together mask and ask for help, it creates the most beautiful friendships.

Joy may seem an unreasonable expectation in your current situation. But I think many of us have the wrong idea about joy. We think it's something that comes effortlessly when everything in your life is going well. But that is the most anti-joy concept I've ever heard. If I have to wait for everything to be perfect to be happy, then it's never going to happen.

Finding joy when your heart aches is exactly what Jesus asked of his disciples. In the 16th chapter of John he speaks about his own coming death, and the persecution his followers will suffer. Serious downer, right? But there are no excuses from Jesus. Instead of focusing on death he says, *"... your sorrow will be turned to joy."* Rather than dwell on persecution he says, *"... your joy no one will take from you."*

Living in joy is a choice. It does not come from having perfect circumstances. Can you think of people who seem to have everything, but are still grouchy? Or, do you know someone who lives joyfully even though their life has been difficult? If all your wishes came true right now, it wouldn't guarantee happiness, would it?

You want to choose joy, but how do you get (and maintain) it when joy seems so distant from your reality? First, ask for it. Jesus continues the joy theme saying, *"Until now you have asked nothing in My name. Ask, and you will receive, that your joy may be full."* John 16:24 (NKJV)

> Finding joy when your heart aches is exactly what Jesus asked of his disciples.

Next, start living it—even if you don't feel it. I know this seems weird, but it's a step of faith. One of my favorite Bible verses is

John 14:27. *"Peace I leave with you; my peace I give you. I do not give to you as the world gives. Do not let your hearts be troubled and do not be afraid."* These words of Jesus remind me that he is with me and puts my worries in perspective. Find encouraging verses in the Bible and memorize them, or post them where you will see them.

Find a friend (or whole support team) that will lift you up and pray with you. When I started teaching this book as a small group Bible study it changed my life. Every parent I've listened to, shared with, and prayed for has expanded my joy more than I would have thought possible. What else can you do?

- Play uplifting songs.

- Read inspirational stories.

- Keep a journal of your joys, successes and blessings.

And don't keep all that to yourself. Make it your mission to lift up the people around you. Joy is reciprocal.

Finally, give thanks to the Lord for his gift of joy. In Luke 10:21 Jesus received joy from the Holy Spirit, and out of that elation came an outpouring of thanks to God. And that is exactly the point with joy. True joy is a miracle. It does not depend on happy circumstances. It is a gift you choose to accept. Let it fill you until it spills over and splashes onto others.

> . . . when I take off my have-it-all-together mask and ask for help, it creates the most beautiful friendships.

Tip 3. Persistently Advocate for Your Child.

The royal official traveled a day's journey and firmly, but respectfully, made his request. The Syrophoenician woman pursued Jesus and would not take no for an answer. Both were rewarded for their persistence and their faith.

Jesus gave at least two more examples of persistence rewarded. In Luke 11:5-10. He tells a story about a persistent friend and ends with these words. *"So I say to you, ask, and it will be given to you; seek and you will find; knock, and it will be opened to you."* (NKJV) He even says it twice to drive the persistency point home; keep asking until you get what you need. In Luke 18:1-8 Jesus reminds us to persevere in our prayers, telling a parable of a woman who pesters a judge until she gets justice. He says, *"... shall God not avenge His own elect who cry out day and night to Him ...?"* (NKJV)

Support is not as far away as you may think, but you do have to open the door to it. Are you working with your spouse or allowing stress to divide you? Are you leaning on family and friends or isolating yourself? Are you angry with the school or church that seems to blame you or your child for causing problems? When it comes to your child, it's easy to be defensive. If you are like me you have developed over-reactive responses to anticipated accusations. But sometimes, with a little patience and effort, those perceived enemies can become your biggest allies.

It became an expected routine to receive a call or email from Caden's new teacher during the first week (sometimes the first day) of school, wanting to schedule a meeting to talk about his behavior. Between fiercely wanting to protect my son, under-standing how difficult it was to work with him, and having no idea how to fix any of it, made these sessions torturous.

I recall one teacher being very frustrated with Caden in her class. I had already cast her in the role of antagonist, but I lis-tened politely, and I did my best to offer suggestions that might help. Part of our agreed-upon solution was that he would check in with her every day after school to review that day's behavior and homework assignments.

By our next meeting that teacher had turned into Caden's biggest cheerleader. In their brief afternoon interactions she had come to know and bond with him. Caden sensed her authentic desire for him to do well, and he put all his effort into doing just that.

Through that experience I learned a lot about myself—how to interact with teachers, but more importantly, I learned what motivated Caden. This armed me with the information I needed to request the kind of teacher my child needed to thrive—which I did every year through elementary school. Even negative inci-dents gave me tools for the future. I learned how to speak up on his behalf with a collaborative, rather than a defensive attitude.

This was educational for Caden as well. He needed to know his parents were going to stand up for him. And through our exam-ple he was learning how to advocate for himself—calmly, respectfully, and persistently. An important part of advocating is knowing when to step back. Depending on your child, the cir-cumstances, and the Lord's guidance, we need to look for opportunities *not* to intervene. We can encourage our kids to find a way to do their best in spite of difficult people and situa-tions. This is real life.

> An important part of advocating is knowing when to step back.

When Caden got his first middle school schedule we compared with friends. A particular teacher was pointed out to us as being very strict and kind of boring. Knowing Caden's distractibility, and low threshold for boredom, we discussed and prayed about whether to try to change his schedule. We felt led to stay out of it. I'm so glad we did. The structure of her classroom worked for him. And because she took a little extra time with him when he needed it, he rose to her high standards.

Teachers, counselors, principals, and other staff involved in your child's education, usually, genuinely want to help. After all, it's in their best interest to see your child's behavior improve and test scores rise. The best thing we can do is give them open lines of communications and support what they're doing at school as much as possible. We can let them know what works at home and build a rapport.

That said, you will need to be an advocate for your child. Stand your ground when you need to—without being argumentative. Remember that the royal official and the Syrophoenician woman made their requests with *respect* and *humility*, but also with *persistence*.

Let's not miss the point that both of those parents made an effort, sacrificed their pride, and reached out in faith. You will almost certainly have to step into uncomfortable zones to advocate for your child. I have asked for help, educated myself, gone to about a million appointments, sacrificed time and money, and even let go of some of my own wants and dreams. Not only *can* you do all this and more, you may find you fight for your child with a sense of purpose. Reach out to Jesus. Take the time to really listen to him, and move forward with faith. It may not be easy, but if you're following God's direction it will definitely be worth it.

Tip 4. Lift Up Your Child.

As Jesus healed Jairus's daughter he took her hand and said, *"Arise."* When he healed the epileptic boy he took his hand and lifted him up. Each of these actions were both Jesus's prayer of healing and a direction he moved them—up.

I adore the simplicity of Jesus's approach in these stories. A prayer can be a single word, or even a simple action. This is something to teach your child about praying on his or her own. Prayers don't have to be long and complicated, just coming from a heart that loves God. Praying for your child is so essential we'll spend a later chapter on it. The example Jesus gives us here is to combine prayer with a tangible move in an upward direction.

Here's a few ways to do that.

- Create opportunities for your child's success and growth.

- Celebrate every achievement, no matter how small.

- Find your child's talents, gifts, abilities, and passions, then nurture them.

For example, as I began to learn more about the condition that specifically affected our family—ADHD—I found some surprising silver linings. Did you know there are beneficial traits that often accompany people with ADHD? They are frequently creative, problem-solving, curious, adventurous, inquisitive, emotionally intuitive, friendly, energetic, and determined. Simply knowing this helped me look for and encourage these traits in my child.

Additionally, each of us has talents and interests. Our son has a beautiful singing voice. We didn't realize this until his last year of Middle School, when he surprised us by getting the lead in the school musical. Seeing him enjoy praise from teachers and peers was pure joy for a mother's heart. It was a success he desperately needed after years of being labeled as "the kid who causes trouble." We have continued to support his interest in music. It has given him a positive outlet, and contributed to his sense of self-worth.

And there's more. We all have spiritual gifts, given by God to help us accomplish his work. Finding how you are gifted can spark a passion to serve—in a way that you truly enjoy. There is nothing more empowering than knowing you're being used by God to do good in the world. Look at the list in Romans 12:6-8 for a quick and easy starting place. The seven gifts listed there are prophecy, serving, teaching, encouraging, giving, leading, and mercy. (A free assessment test is available at www.spiritual-giftsworkbook.com.)

I prayed over this list with my son in mind. I talked with him about it. Looking at the times he was energized and naturally in his element, we decided the spiritual gift of giving made sense. He has always been happy to share whatever he has with others. He doesn't worry about money because he can always find a way to make more. One summer he organized the kids in our neighborhood to work shifts at a lemonade stand. He purchased supplies, kept the books, distributed profits, and had a blast. By the age of 16 he had added dishwasher, retirement home server, lifeguard, and carhop to his resume.

Parents, you need to take the time to acknowledge or discover your own talents, strengths, and spiritual gifts too. God created and equipped you uniquely. Focusing on those, and giving God gratitude for them, can put fresh wind in your sails for your journey.

Having successes to celebrate is an important part of every child's life. But, if your family is dealing with real challenges, make it your mission to lift up your child *every day*. I found that when I do this it changes the tone in our house for the better. When I forget to encourage him, I have noticed that my son looks for affirmation in destructive and unhealthy ways. I can't overstate how important this is. No matter how deep you have to dig, even if it seems like an insignificant thing to mention, even if compliments don't come easy to you—lift up your child! It is what Jesus demonstrated.

> No matter how deep you have to dig, even if it seems like an insignificant thing to mention, even if compliments don't come easy to you—lift up your child!

Make a list of your child's gifts, talents, abilities, passions, personality traits, and anything else you love about him or her. Talk to them about how God created them perfectly, to accomplish a particular mission. Let them know you can't wait to see how God will work through their one-of-a-kind life to do great things.

There is one more kind of "lifting up" we can do as parents: Point our children toward Jesus. Share the following concepts with your child, letting him or her know that Jesus is talking directly to them.

We can share Jesus's words about salvation. *"For God so loved the world that he gave his one and only Son, that whoever believes in him shall not perish but have eternal life."* John 3:16. (TLB)

We can teach them that Jesus loves children. *"... Let the little children come to Me, and do not forbid them ..."* Luke 18:16. (NKJV)

We can comfort them with the promise they will never be alone. *"... I am with you always ..."* Matt. 28:20 (NKJV)

We assure them that they are chosen by Jesus. *"You did not choose Me, but I chose you and appointed you ..."* John 15:16 (NKJV)

We can remind them that Jesus will calm their fears. *"... My peace I give to you; ... Let not your heart be troubled, neither let it be afraid."* John 14:27 (NKJV)

In his own words, Jesus gets to the heart of our needs. It's never too early to start sharing these promises with your child. These are tools he or she can use now and for a lifetime. Even if they are too young. Even if they don't truly comprehend them— teach them anyway. Jesus's words will provide encouragement for your whole family. Let his words fill the air in your home, and trust the Holy Spirit to bring them to life.

Tip 5. Go Your Way.

"Give her something to eat." After raising a girl from the dead, Jesus gives her parents this oddly mundane suggestion. To both the Syrophoenician woman and the royal official he heals their

children and says, *"Go your way."* In his succinct way, he encourages them to get back to living their everyday life. He didn't bring healing so they could be a side-show for gawkers and gossips. The same is true for our children. You may have to shake off those that judge, mock, or discourage and find your own normal.

> . . . shake off those that judge, mock, or discourage and find your own normal.

Jesus himself knew what it was like to be made fun of. *"If the world hates you, you know that it hated Me before it hated you."* John 15:18. (NKJV) His simple command to, *"Go your way,"* encourages us to find our worth in the love of Jesus. If you are focused on God's direction for your family, it doesn't matter what anyone else thinks.

Your family may not look perfect to outsiders. (It probably doesn't look perfect to the insiders either.) But I can tell you this, what is normal for you won't be the same for others. The road you travel with your family will have a different view and require some different luggage, but the destination is the same. We're working toward a loving family relationship, hoping to raise our kids to be the best humans they are capable of being. I'm always looking for just the right items to pack into our family's bag. These are tools and ideas collected along the journey, to be pulled out when needed.

When my son was ten we went to see comedian Tim Hawkins with another family. It was a fantastic show. At the end, we rubbed our laugh-weary sides and cheeks as we heard the announcement that Tim would be signing autographs by the stage. Caden said, "I'm going!" And he zipped through the exiting crowd like a salmon swimming upstream. By the time

Caden got to the line it looked like an hour wait. It was late, a school night, and we didn't drive. The other family said they couldn't stay. My husband went to retrieve Caden and a sense of doom began to build in my mind.

Even from the back of the auditorium I could see negotiations were not going well. Caden was digging in his heels. As Roger tried to keep the situation from escalating, my friend turned to me and said, "You just need to tell him no, and leave."

It was good advice—for 95% of kids. I wanted to tell her that if this didn't go down exactly the right way, Caden would flip out and go running out of the building and into the dark. We might spend the next few hours talking to the police and combing a neighborhood we didn't know, for a kid that would hide until he was good-and-ready to be found. Instead I gave her a hug and said, "Thank you, but you just don't understand." I knew her advice came from a genuine and caring heart. But what works for most families is not our normal.

In these moments we have to be more creative, more patient, and definitely pray on the fly. Which is what we did in that situation. Roger handled it with the kind of wisdom that can only come from a combination of prayer and years of experience with our specific child. That night Caden's control was stretched to near the breaking point, but it held. Roger was able to talk him into leaving on his own terms, rather than throwing him over a shoulder and carrying him to the car. The ride home was awkward enough, but if you let it, these situations can actually strengthen friendships. That other family is still among our most treasured friends.

> . . . what works for most families is not our normal.

49

Yes, This is Your Calling

When Jesus spoke to each of those parents in the Bible I think he knew that a parent and child relationship is a special thing. Most people choose their life's work, and while they may have great passion for it, they could also walk away from it. Parenting is different. You may or may not have chosen it, but it is nevertheless a calling filled with passion, hard work, and a lifetime commitment.

Jesus promises the Holy Spirit will teach us what we need to know and equip us for our calling. Most of you wonderful parents have probably always understood that parenting is your calling, but I'm a little slow. I spent a lot of time waiting for God to show me the big plan he has for my life. I was so determined to find it I almost missed it.

I was sitting next to my ten-year-old Caden during a church service. He turned to me and said, "mom," in a whisper loud enough for a six-seat radius to hear. But this time I didn't hiss at him to be quiet. He called me "mom," and it pierced my heart in a new way. In that instant I felt Jesus say, *"I have given you a new name. Like Peter or Abraham, the name is suited for the calling."*

When Jesus changed Simon's name to Peter he was calling him to a new purpose. Peter means rock. Jesus knew he would become the rock on which his church would be built. (John 1:42) God also changed Abram to Abraham, calling him the father of a multitude. (Gen. 17:5) Sari, meaning quarrelsome, became Sarah, meaning princess. (Gen. 17:15) Jacob, meaning the deceiver, was given the name Israel, as one who prevails with God. (Gen. 32:28.) Each name came with new significance, new blessings, and new responsibilities. From the moment you are first called mother or father you have been given a sacred mission.

Take another look at the five tips. But instead of viewing them as difficult goals, think of them as encouragement from the Lord Jesus. He is equipping you for the very special calling he placed in your life.

1. Have faith and believe.
2. Do not be afraid. Do not weep.
3. Persistently advocate for your child.
4. Lift up your child.
5. Go your way.

Contrary to the age-old joke, we do have something of an instruction book for parenting. The Bible doesn't teach you how to change a diaper, but it does offer guidance. Jesus said, *"But the Helper, the Holy Spirit, whom the Father will send in My name, He will teach you all things, and bring to your remembrance all things that I said to you."* John 14:26 (NKJV) So we become students, seeking wisdom, and learning how to rely on Jesus's words and examples.

> From the moment you are first called mother or father you have been given a sacred mission.

Chapter 4

Desperate Parents Club, Twenty-First Centrury Edition

As I mentioned in chapter two, we are not looking at other parents' stories to compare their children to ours, but to identify with their turning points and learn how to rely on Jesus in our desperation. It's not so hard to relate to the parents Jesus interacted with in the Bible. The love of a parent for their child is a timeless phenomenon. Two thousand years later we are still losing sleep, seeking answers, shedding tears, and fighting for the best for our children. And Jesus is still available, ready to lighten our burdens when we ask.

The definition of *desperate parent* is as unique as each of us. I have had the pleasure of meeting many other parents navigating their own desperate parenting situations. Every story is both heartbreaking and beautiful. Each mom or dad struggling to do the best for their child is my soul sister or brother—no matter how different the details of our lives. And every success and moment of joy is a reason to celebrate together.

The parents featured in this chapter are dealing with modern circumstances, but their need for Jesus transcends any date, location, or experience. They have graciously allowed me to share their stories with the hope that you will be encouraged to trust God in your darkest moments, and will be inspired to share your story with someone else.

Kirsten's Story

Kirsten and Paul sent their son Neal off to college like most parents, filled with pride and dreams for his future. Despite a learning disability (dysgraphia) and an ADD diagnosis, he had graduated from high school as an honor student. They talked to him about the challenges that would come with college, but also the great experiences he would have with marching band, campus events, and new friends.

When Neal came home for Christmas break Kirsten observed some concerning issues. Her six-foot-four son had always been thin, but his gaunt face and protruding shoulders took her by surprise. Usually sweet and affectionate, he was now withdrawn and uncommunicative. He stayed up until 3am and slept until mid-day. But what they really needed to discuss was his academic probation.

To help him succeed in the next semester they changed some courses and hired an academic coach to meet with him once per week online. Kirsten also started paying closer attention to his behaviors—as much as she could from a distance. She checked his meal plan charges, stalked his location on a cell phone app, and quizzed his roommate about how he was spending his time.

By spring break she had reached a distressing conclusion. He was addicted to computer gaming. He left his room only to go to class—though his grades were falling rapidly. He turned down all invitations from friends to go out. He typically ate no more than once a day. He became primarily nocturnal. He was pale, mean and nasty, and motivated by nothing beyond gaming. Though he wasn't ready to admit it, he was suffering both mentally and physically.

Kirsten decided to let him finish the semester while she took the time to research options and get her husband on board. The latter part took some convincing, but by this time the problems were undeniable. When Neal came home for the summer they were ready to act.

All of that was the easy part. It was about to get a lot more painful—starting with an intervention.

Trying to find the right balance of tough and love, they laid out their concerns and a plan to move forward. He would not be going back to college in the fall. If he wanted to live in their house he would need to meet with doctors and therapists to address his addiction and follow their recommendations. After initial denial and resistance, he agreed to the plan.

At that time the World Health Organization had not yet classified digital or video gaming as a disorder. There were very few experts or treatment options available in this emerging field—and insurance covered none of it. A rehabilitation center was cost-prohibitive so they focused on therapy. Finding a psychiatrist with some experience in this area they began sessions that sometimes involved the whole family, including their younger son.

The next year was an extreme test for all of them. Therapy will only work if the person works with it. There are physical withdrawal symptoms for a gaming addiction like with any substance. And, like many addicts, Neal went down the road of lies and deception to get his particular "fix." Kirsten and Paul often disagreed about how to help him. The fighting, yelling, and stress affected everyone in the house.

Kirsten's guiding principle was to do anything necessary to put Neal on a path toward health and eventual independence. She often felt like that made her the bad guy. Though it was the hardest thing she's ever done she stood her ground and made the tough decisions. She knew he hated her for it. She wondered if she was giving up ever having a good relationship with her son again.

> She was honest with God about the battery of emotions that assaulted her.

Where was Jesus in all of this? As a longtime Christian, of course Kirsten prayed for Neal. And she was honest with God about the battery of emotions that assaulted her. Some days she got angry with God. Some days she felt overwhelmed with guilt that everything was her fault. Occasionally she mourned the loss of her dreams for Neal. And sometimes she was simply grateful that they weren't dealing with something worse, like an illegal drug addiction or a fatal disease.

When Kirsten joined a *5 Tips from Jesus for Desperate Parents* small group study, two of the tips particularly struck home for her. The first was to persistently advocate for your child. This was her job, her reason for living. Knowing that Jesus encouraged parents to fight for their children reinforced her determination on behalf of her son.

Go your way (also understood as, find your normal) was the other tip she needed to hear. On one level it freed her from the feeling that everyone was judging how she handled their situation. On another level she realized that she had been judging others' parenting choices. This new perspective helped her release judgment to focus on things that really matter.

Three years after Neal's intervention things are improving, but by no means complete. He works and takes classes at a community college. For a couple of years he lived in his parents' basement—paying a modest rent. Then he moved into a house with roommates. He's learning to reintroduce technology into his life—in moderation. He is no longer full of hate and self-destruction. His family and friends are beginning to see the guy they know and love emerge again. And his mother? She's prepared for the long haul, no matter what that looks like.

Brandon and Pam's Story

Brandon was stationed in Italy with his wife Pam and their three young boys when they got the diagnosis. Their middle son, two-and-half-year-old Emmitt, had autism spectrum disorder. They were stunned and unsure what to do. At that time the only reference they had for autism was the movie "Rainman," and that didn't represent their son at all.

Initially they didn't want this news to affect Brandon's job and the life they were building in Italy, but after a few days of research they discovered that consistent, long-term therapy would offer him the best life possible. It made more sense to head back to the States right away. Within two weeks they were packing.

Years passed. God blessed them with another child—a daughter. Brandon and Pam never stopped striving for the best for all of their children. As they grew, their other kids supported their brother with autism, developing understanding and empathy for anyone with special needs.

Anyone that took the time to get to know Emmitt grew to love him. His kind heart, love of animals, and compassion for anyone sick or suffering was evident. His math skills put him at the top of his class. He was generally compliant and happy. In some respects he was their easiest kid.

But fear was an enemy that hovered close. Emmitt was a runner and managed to escape multiple times. His parents were constantly on guard, but he seemed to get away at unexpected moments. On more than one occasion they had to ask others for help finding him. They missed many of their other children's events for fear of him running off. Another worry came from wondering what would happen to him when they got too old to take care of him. Would he be able to make an independent life for himself?

There were also moments of frustration: When he smeared poop all over his room when he was supposed to be taking a nap. They felt judged: When he had a meltdown in the middle of a store. They felt isolated: When they weren't invited to parties (even family gatherings) because he was unpredictable, or his diet was an inconvenience. They were embarrassed: When he tried to take off his clothes in public because he spilled a few drops of water on them.

Brandon and Pam were disappointed when their church's children's ministry director started making excuses for not allowing Emmitt to attend church. So that the rest of the family could go to church, often Brandon would attend an early service while Pam stayed home with Emmitt, then they would switch off so Pam could go to the second service. That lasted a couple of years, until a job opportunity moved them to Kansas.

They found a new church that seemed to be a great fit, but it ended up being their biggest heartbreak. The church had a wonderful special needs program for Emmitt, but the children's ministry did not have the flexibility to allow him to participate with peers, serve others, or attend activities outside of the special needs group. For instance, Emmitt loved to do motions with songs and wanted to help with the kids' worship team—like other kids his age. Brandon and Pam appealed to the children's pastor without success. When Emmitt wanted to go to summer church camp, they brought their request to the children's pastor again. They even offered to find a personal aid to accompany him. But he was denied because, "That extra person might take up a spot that another child needed so they could learn about Jesus." They couldn't help but ask, what about Emmitt's need to learn about Jesus?

That particular pastor made it very difficult for Brandon and Pam to advocate for their son. When alone with him their requests were uncompromisingly refused. Around other leaders in the church he made himself out as graciously accommodating. Brandon and Pam felt labeled as troublemakers. Their family had become deeply involved with their church over five years, but the situation had become toxic. They made the tough decision to leave.

For Brandon and Pam, it was not a single moment that brought them to the point of desperation. There have been many times when they've cried out to Jesus for help. Every time fear stole their peace, or injustice mocked their pain, they had a chance to practice reliance on God. Jesus's encouragement to *"Have faith,"* and *"Do not be afraid, just believe."* were reminders they lived by. They trusted God to provide exactly what they needed. And you know what? He did!

God provided a church where everyone in the family was welcomed. The SOAR Special Needs Ministry at their new church cared about Emmitt's specific abilities, his dignity, and his relationship with God. They supported his parents with a respite night, resources, and friendship. They provided understanding and programs for siblings of kids with special needs. In retrospect Brandon and Pam can see God's guidance. Without the challenge at their previous church they would have stayed right where they were, and missed out on their next adventure.

As they continued to navigate the ups and downs of their particular life, they heard the call to minister to other struggling families. With their children now in their teens and twenties Brandon and Pam have wisdom to share, prayers to offer, and encouragement to extend. Whether it's through moms playing Bunco, or dads over breakfast, or a social media support group, they minister to hundreds of parents on a regular basis. And in a true answer to prayer, they are seeing those parents grow in faith and begin reaching out to others in an ever-expanding radius of grace.

> Every time fear stole their peace, or injustice mocked their pain, they had a chance to practice reliance on God.

Jarell's Story

Fatherhood. Jarell had wanted to be a father since he was a boy. He also wanted to be a teacher, but that didn't happen in the usual sense. Instead he joined the Air Force. He has been on several tours of duty and continues to serve in the Air National Guard and Reserves. When not in military service he is a speaker, comedian, consultant, part time youth pastor, volunteer at juvenile justice centers, and Youth for Christ, and founder of two non-profits. One is Our Gathering Place, a ministry that organizes dinner events for families with special needs so they can enjoy an evening out surrounded by love and support rather than stares and judgement. The other is #HopeHood, which utilizes the entertainment arts to bring hope to the homeless, disabled, and neighbors in need.

And in case that isn't enough, he also teaches boxing.

Jarell became a father when he married Kinesha (a writer, speaker, and the chef and organizer of Our Gathering Place) who came to their marriage with a four-year-old son named John. Jarell loved John immediately and longed to be his father. But the boy was focused on his biological father—a man who stepped in and out of his life over the years. Jarell understood that need but didn't give up praying for genuine connection with his stepson. He settled in for the long and patient approach.

Soon, fatherhood expanded to include three more children: Karia, a tall, strong, and beautiful girl who likes playing with makeup and mud equally, Jeremiah, an affectionate lady's man who speaks mostly with his eyes and smile, and Karley, a bright and joyful girl, destined to be a performer. Each child broadened Jarell's heart and drove him to be the best father he could be.

Karia and Jeremiah were each diagnosed with autism, bringing new challenges and new opportunities to their family. Jarell loved all his children well. As busy as he was, he made time to be fully present in their lives. But fear threatened to steal his joy. Sometimes his unpredictable income was stressful. Sometimes he doubted that his stepson would ever fully accept him. Sometimes he worried he didn't fit the ideals of fatherhood. Sometimes the weight of responsibility was overwhelming. The fear of failing his family plagued him.

Jarell has a theory that God can give us fears to put us on our guard, to help us plan or act, and make us productive. So, he got real with God about his doubts and fears. God answered with a revelation. Having kids makes you a dad. Being a father is to be named and called by God. Many men have kids without really being a father. God called Jarell and gifted him to be a father in the way that God is a father. He longs for his children—even if they reject him. He invests in his children—even if the world can't see their potential. He corrects his children in a way that meets them where they are in the moment. He loves his children—sacrificially, protectively, enthusiastically. Always.

As Jarell let go of his own expectations, and stopped worrying about others' expectations, he felt the peace of knowing he was doing what he was called to do. It wasn't his own strength or wisdom, but the never-failing guidance of the Lord that got him through difficulties. This insight is what he models for his children. He teaches them to be transformed by knowing Jesus and step into what he calls God's big hope and big future!

Which brings us back to Jarell's relationship with his stepson John. Jarell's persistent prayers and consistent love bonded them over time. Now in college, John is close with both of his parents. He listens, thinks deeply, and respects their advice—because he has seen them live what they teach. He is now paving his own path toward "God's big hope and big future" that his father is always talking about.

> "Having kids makes you a dad. Being a father is to be named and called by God."

Carrie's Story

When Carrie held her newborn daughter for the first time she already knew Mackenzie had Down syndrome. After finding out through an amniocentesis test, she processed the news in stages. She wept, lost sleep, and worried about a million things. She took some time to grieve and try to let go of her expectations. But Carrie's faith and optimism didn't let her stay low for long. She and her husband reached out to a couple at their church who had a child with Down syndrome. With friends to pray with and learn from, they looked forward to a future with the gift God had given them.

Faith, optimism, and a support team are great tools to start any parenting journey. These new parents had no idea how much they were going to need those tools—and so much more. In her first year Mackenzie struggled to keep food down due to an esophageal stricture and GERD. For the next couple years chronic constipation would trouble her. Around five years old she began displaying inexplicably aggressive behavior. More tests revealed a thyroid issue.

And then, cancer. When she was six, Mackenzie was diagnosed with acute lymphoblastic leukemia. For the next two and a half years she suffered through chemotherapy, gastrostomy tubes, countless blood tests, and hospital stays.

Thank God, the treatments worked. With the leukemia in remission the family began constructing what their normal life would look like. That's when Mackenzie's behavior became problematic. More doctors, more tests, and a new list of diagnoses came in rapid succession. ADHD, ODD, hearing loss in one ear, poor spatial awareness, and scoliosis were all added to Mackenzie's chart by the time she was ten years old.

And then, divorce. Like so many parents in prolonged, high pressure situations, their marriage fell apart. Even though they were Christians, even though they both loved their daughter fiercely, the relentless stress took its toll. Carrie became Mackenzie's primary guardian, with her ex-husband coming to visit a couple times a week.

Life didn't stop to let Carrie mourn her marriage. Mackenzie's medical complications continued, adding Graves' disease when she was eleven, and a spine fusion surgery when she was twelve. The recent need to add glasses to her accessories seemed almost a relief from the severity of previous events.

How does a parent cope with that kind of onslaught? The culmination of her daughter's medical issues brought Carrie to her knees repeatedly, asking God for wisdom. She appreciated the support of friends who tried to understand, but she still felt isolated. One of her biggest sources of inspiration came from Mackenzie herself.

The child had suffered through the pain and confusion of endless treatments, but Carrie marveled at her daughter's delight to see her nurse and doctor friends every time they went to the hospital. Every Halloween Mackenzie dressed up as her favorite oncology nurse. Most of the time she had a smile on her face and wanted everyone around her to be happy.

Seeing how her daughter could brighten lives reminded Carrie that God has a plan for everyone. Every experience each person goes through provides a unique platform to tell others about Jesus. This concept strengthened her faith. She put her family into Jesus's hands and trusted him to use their situation for good. That doesn't mean it was easy. Each new diagnosis brought a fresh struggle, but also an opportunity. As she practiced leaning on God through her desperation, the roots of her faith grew deeper, the knowledge that she was not alone grew stronger, and the wisdom of the Holy Spirit led her as she advocated for her child.

> Seeing how her daughter could brighten lives reminded Carrie that God has a plan for everyone.

One particular instance happened when Mackenzie was in the hospital with leukemia. A G-Tube had been inserted. Even though they kept increasing medications and trying to push more fluids into her, she kept throwing up. A young med student said they were going to increase everything again. But Carrie couldn't ignore the conviction that something else was wrong. As she prayed, the solution to the problem appeared in her mind like an image. With the confidence of the Holy Spirit supporting her, she stood up and said she thought the balloon of the G-Tube was covering the opening of Mackenzie's intestines. They needed to look at that first. He disagreed. She lost her cool and said she would rip the machine out of the wall if he turned it on again. He complied. And guess what? That was exactly what was causing the problem.

Carrie is not suggesting you fight with the doctors, therapists, or educators in your child's life. She believes God gives us his Spirit when we accept him as our savior. If you're continually praying for your child and something seems wrong, it is absolutely appropriate to say no, stop, or wait until the options can be fully vetted. Trust what you know about your child and ask the Lord for guidance.

> "... if something seems wrong, it is absolutely appropriate to say no, stop, or wait until the options can be fully vetted."

As Carrie looks forward it's easy to find things to worry about. But she has learned that worrying makes zero difference to the outcome. Instead, she releases fear to God so she can focus on the things she can control. She celebrates the wins—no matter how small. She prays for wisdom to raise Mackenzie, and meet her where she is at the moment. She encourages other families to embrace their unique normal, not the expectations of the world. She would assure you, the challenges of life can feel over-whelming, but God is there. Always.

John's Story

John wrote three suicide letters. One to his son, one to his wife, and one to his parents. He wasn't sure he would go through with it, but he couldn't see a way out. Stress, failure, despair, and loneliness pressed in on him like four walls of a shrinking room, while the voice in his mind judged him mercilessly. "You have no job. You're failing as a father. Your wife no longer respects you. No one cares if you're around."

The truth was inescapable. He had lost his job as an elementary school teacher. Bills were piling up and he was unable to find a new job that would work around his son's needs. His son Christopher had been diagnosed with autism many years before. Chris was mostly non-verbal with minor motor limita-tions, but he had good therapists and was making progress. John loved his son desperately, but often he didn't know how to help him. His marriage was crumbling under the pressure of dwin-dling finances and caring for their son. The knowledge that they couldn't exist on his wife's teacher salary alone for very long ticked a relentless reminder of his failure. His stress was escalat-ing as quickly as his confidence was plummeting. Perhaps worst of all, he felt utterly alone.

The process of writing those letters unearthed the pain he had been trying to bury and forced him to face it. He did not go through with his plan, but emerged knowing something had to change. A friend had recently suggested John try out a men's group at her church. He had nothing to lose, so he gave it a shot. On the very first night someone asked him to share his story. The circle of men listened and cared. Their encouraging words rang louder than the judgmental voice in his head. And when they shared Jesus's gift of salvation with him, he grasped it like a lifeline. He believed Jesus died for his sins, asked God to forgive him, and made a commitment to follow him.

His wife began to see a change in him. They started attending church together and before long she became a Christian as well. They found support and programs for their son through the church. They found friends who encouraged them on this new path. Slowly, they began to heal as a family.

As John learned to see himself through Jesus's eyes, he found his true worth. He did find a new teaching job but realized that wasn't the source of his value. He put his heart into advocating for his son. It turned out he was not only good at it, but he enjoyed the education and interaction with others as they worked together to help Chris live his best life. After a time of receiving the encouragement he needed, he was inspired to pour into the lives of other dads of kids with special needs. If his experiences could help even one person, he felt it would all be worth it.

He started small and hasn't stopped yet. He looked for opportunities for one-on-one encouragement. He started a group for other parents like himself. He organized a neighborhood meet-up for dads of kids with special needs. He started writing a blog. He volunteered as a Special Father's Network mentor for the 21st Century Dads organization. He became a contributing writer for national organizations like Key Ministry and Hope Anew. On top of all that, he was consulting—both as an educator and a special needs advocate.

Life was hitting a good stride when eleven-year-old Christopher suffered a grand mal seizure. A series of tests revealed a brain malformation at the base of his skull. He was sent home on seizure medication with a date scheduled for brain surgery. On the day of the surgery John walked his son into the hospital with a supportive arm around his back. That's when he felt the trembling. His child couldn't express what he was feeling with words, but he understood enough to be terrified. Powerlessness swept over John like a monstrous wave, stealing his breath and threatening to pull his feet out from under him. He fought the current long enough to reassure his son, see him sedated for the surgery, and then find the hospital chapel before collapsing.

He reached out to God in total surrender. What else could he do? He begged God to take anything he'd been given—any grace, any blessing—and transfer it to his son to heal him. Even in his desperation, John recognized that this crisis felt different than the one he had weathered seven years before. He was filled with gratitude for his relationship with Jesus, and the support of friends who flooded heaven with their prayers and surrounded his family with love.

> You might think handling a crisis gets easier after going through one or two.

Christopher's surgery was successful. They even began to see some improvements in his motor skills which could be attributed to the procedure. John threw himself back into his calling whole-heartedly. He realized he was gifted as a relationship-builder and networker; God was placing him in a position to connect people and ministries. He continued to find ways to share his story and encourage other dads—whether as a mentor, an event speaker, or podcast guest.

You might think handling a crisis gets easier after going through one or two. John would tell you it doesn't. When the unexpected knocks you down, the pain is just as raw as ever. You still instinctively react with anger, bitterness, and depression.

Unexpectedly, John's wife served him with divorce papers. He didn't handle it like a perfect Christian. He got angry—sometimes at his wife, sometimes at God. He acknowledged his shortcomings in their marriage and tried to find a way to work things out, but her mind was set.

When John was honest with himself, he realized his real struggle was the shame of feeling like a fraud. He had counseled others about how to keep marriages together while navigating the stresses of a special-needs family. His advice had always been to lean on God. He wondered how he was supposed to explain that, and if anyone would ever listen to him again. He still has bad days, but faith and friends have helped him surrender what he can't control. He has stopped trying to explain it. It is simply this: We live in a broken world.

John is more determined than ever to be a part of what God is doing and knows he can encourage people with the hope that Jesus offers. That is enough for him. He tells himself the same thing he would tell you … or his son. God wants to use everybody—even if you think you're not worthy, or skilled, or your reputation is tarnished. John will keep walking through the doors God opens, knowing he is part of something special. Learn more about John's expanding ministry at www.johnfelageller.com

John and his ex-wife are co-parenting well. The unexpected blessing of shared custody is this: Every moment he spends with his son is a treasure. Every smile is a gift. Even the occasional challenge is welcome, because it's clear in Christopher's eyes—he loves being with his dad just as much.

If you'd like to read more desperate parent stories, go to www.5TipsfromJesus.com. Do you have a desperate parent story that could inspire others? Submit your information through the website. Think about it. Maybe someone out there needs to hear how you learned to rely on God through your experiences.

> "God wants to use everybody—even if you think you're not worthy, or skilled, or your reputation is tarnished."

# Chapter 5

What Exactly Are We Fighting?

Fair warning: We are going to talk about the devil. Maybe you don't believe in an evil spirit at work in the world. Are you uncomfortable with the idea? Don't want to think about it? Fair enough. I appreciate honesty, which is why I'm being up-front about the direction of this chapter. I will explain why I do believe and why it is relevant for a desperate parent. You don't have to agree, but I have a challenge for you as you read this chapter: Find at least one concept that can be applied to your life.

Let's start with the name. Even writing the name Satan makes me a little cringy—so does the name Hitler. There are strong associations with those names. My default is to avoid things that make me uncomfortable, but sometimes, eventually, you have to face them. Let me explain my perspective through my son's diagnosis.

The term ADHD has some baggage. Some say it's a bad idea to label kids as having attention-deficit/hyperactivity disorder. That may be true. I spent a lot of time trying to skirt around it or call it something else, for fear of damaging my child's self-esteem, or giving others preconceived ideas about him. Eventually I decided that was disingenuous—for me. I prefer to name it and address it. I don't want to fear it. I don't want my child to see ADHD as either a cause for shame or an excuse for bad behavior. A challenge, yes. And, to be honest, I think it's a situation the devil tries to take full advantage of.

Which brings us to the nature of evil. The difference between what is difficult and what is evil may be a little blurry. Let me be clear; I don't think my child's ADHD comes from the devil. I feel like I need to say that again. ADHD is *not* Satanic, demonic possession, a curse, or punishment from God. Debates rage about the causes of ADHD. I'm not smart enough to weigh in with an answer, but this I do know: I've seen how God can use my son's unique combination of gifts, abilities and personality for good—*including* some of the traits that come with ADHD.

Think about your particular situation. Is it possible that the devil sees your difficulties and twists them into an opportunity to destroy God's plans? Evil targets families that are already struggling, shooting arrows of failure, anger, blame, despair, and stress in their direction. We need to ask ourselves if we're passively letting those arrows hit their mark.

Why does it matter? Once I decided to take Jesus's word seriously, I could no longer skip over his warnings about the devil. Jesus not only acknowledges the existence of Satan, he teaches us how to combat the evil and destruction he intends. If we know the enemy and his nature then we can better protect ourselves and our families.

> Evil targets families that are already struggling, shooting arrows of failure, anger, blame, despair, and stress in their direction. We need to ask ourselves if we're passively letting those arrows hit their mark.

A Tale of Two Disciples

I noticed that Jesus talked about the devil specifically in regards to two of his followers. Compare Judas and Peter. These two men provide a contrast to illustrate how the enemy tries to target us. Perhaps we can learn what works (or doesn't) through their stories.

Let's start with Judas Iscariot—the ideal disciple. Wait, what? He was an ideal disciple? It's true. History has cast him as the ultimate villain for betraying Jesus with a kiss. But the Bible indicates he was a respected and active member of Jesus's ministry. Not even the other disciples saw the betrayal coming.

Jesus called Judas to join him, just as he did the other disciples. Judas was sent out to preach, heal, and cast out demons. He had responsibility over the ministry funds, collecting donations, providing for the practical needs of their group and distributing to the needy. Jesus prayed over Judas—loved him.

At his last supper Jesus said, *"one of you will betray me."* The disciples looked around unbelieving, wondering who could do such a thing? Surely not one of the band of brothers sitting around the table. They knew each other well. Even as Jesus singled Judas out and sent him to do what he was going to do, they still gave him the benefit of the doubt, thinking he must be going to give money to the poor.

It is only retrospectively, as the writers of the New Testament add their foreshadowing comments about Judas, that we read his character as evil from the beginning. In this way we discover that Judas had been embezzling from ministry funds. (John 12:3-8) We are reminded with every mention of his name that he will betray Jesus or that he was in league with Satan.

Rather than believing he was born evil, it makes more sense to me that it was a gradual descent. I think Judas was truly passionate about Jesus, but he was ambitious. Jesus had the potential to overthrow an oppressive government and Judas had grand plans. Like a campaign manager for the hot new candidate, Judas was going to push Jesus onto a throne.

The problem for Judas was that Jesus wouldn't cooperate with that plan. Jesus's throne was not of this world and Judas never made peace with that. Was Judas bad from the beginning? I think not. Did he have a choice, or a chance for forgiveness and salvation? I think we all do.

I bet he didn't plan to embezzle. The temptation to steal probably grew out of justification and opportunity. I bet he didn't plan to betray Jesus until near the end. Perhaps his frustration at Jesus's lack of ambition hardened his heart. When he betrayed Jesus, maybe he saw the opportunity to push Jesus into a corner (and make some bank) so he took it, hoping Jesus would come out of that corner fighting. Regardless, he sold Jesus for 30 pieces of silver, leading soldiers to make the arrest, and betraying him with a kiss.

Did Judas ever love Jesus? Matthew 27 says when Judas realized Jesus was condemned to death he returned the money and hung himself. What does that tell you? Did Jesus love Judas? I think Jesus gave him every opportunity to change his path. Even as Judas kissed him, Jesus called him friend.

What went wrong?

Shelf that question for a moment and look at Simon Peter. Unlike Judas, who seemed to have it all together, Peter was an apparent mess. He is a study in contradictions. He had enough faith to jump into the sea to walk to Jesus. Then he got distracted by the storm and Jesus had to rescue him. He declared that Jesus was the Son of God in Matthew 16:16. Then, just a few verses later Jesus rebukes him. *"But He turned and said to Peter,*

'Get behind Me, Satan! You are an offense to Me, for you are not mindful of the things of God, but the things of men.'" (NKJV) Peter violently cuts off a soldier's ear to protect Jesus. Then, only hours later, he denies he even knows Jesus.

At the last supper Jesus says to Simon Peter, *"Simon, Simon! Indeed, Satan has asked for you, that he may sift you as wheat. But I have prayed for you, that your faith should not fail; and when you have returned to Me, strengthen your brethren."* (Luke 22:31-32 NKJV) He flat out tells him that the devil had plans to take over his life, but prayer kept him away. Jesus showed complete confidence in Peter's faith, not only to master himself, but to strengthen other Christians.

But first Peter had to hit a low point. After predicting Judas would betray him, Jesus predicted that Peter would deny him. Peter protested, promising to stay by him even to death. But that same night he swore he didn't even know who Jesus was—three times! On that dark night it certainly seemed Satan had won over both men. (Mark 14:27-31 and 66-72)

Let's compare. At the last supper, Luke 23:3 says, *"Then Satan entered Judas..."* Jesus gave Judas a chance to change his plans, but he was in too deep. He rejected The Lord and allowed Satan to take over. Peter and Judas were both Jesus's disciples. Within a few verses we find that they were both hounded by the devil. One succumbed to it and one did not.

What made the difference?

What about prayer? Prayer is powerful, right? But it had to take more than prayer. Jesus himself prayed for Judas as he did for all his disciples. (John 17:6-26) Jesus calls Judas, "lost." He wanted a relationship, but Judas rejected him. Judas found it easier to join the dark side. It offered the illusion of power. That power lasted mere hours. Satan used Judas and left him in a void of utter weakness and self-loathing. How did Peter resist that pull?

To people watching Jesus's inner group it might have appeared that Judas had it under control. He was the good, holy, and organized disciple. Peter was the unstable one. He often lost his struggles to do the right thing. But that is not the same as being taken over by Satan. In fact, I'd say struggling against something is the opposite of succumbing to it. So, what did Peter have that Judas did not?

Strength made the difference. Fighting made the difference.

That is a concept I can get on board with as a parent fighting for my son, and as I teach my son to fight the temptations of the devil. In fact, as this concept clarified for me, I was able to actually thank God for my son's natural tendency to fight against everything and everyone. I never thought I'd say that.

> . . . struggling against something is the opposite of succumbing to it.

But I Thought Fighting Was a Bad Thing.

It's the enemy's nature to kill, steal and destroy. However, in that same verse, Jesus counters, *"I have come that they may have life, and that they may have it more abundantly."* (John 10:10 NKJV) There's nothing about the chaos of our struggles that feels like abundant life. I Corinthians 14:33 says, *"For God is not the author of confusion but of peace....*" (NKJV) That leaves me with a pretty clear idea where the attack is coming from. Plan of action: Have defensive and offensive strategies to protect your family.

I am a peace-loving person. The previous paragraph uses the type of war words that make me uncomfortable. As a Christian culture we often use battle cries to incite passion, and I have often dismissed that as not in tune with the God of peace. I didn't want to believe that the devil needed to be battled. And that is *exactly* where the devil wanted me.

I was comfortable with my "peaceful" perspective. But, whether I knew what to call it or not, I was struggling under spiritual attacks. Then, as God so often does, he made it personal for me—teaching me the nuances between peace and spiritual warfare. It started when a wise man told me I should teach my son about the armor of God. Thanks Dad. It's among the best advice you've ever given me.

I read Eph. 6:10-20 to my eight-year-old son and it led to an amazing discussion. I have recreated our conversation from memory, combining two or three separate discussions on the subject. I let his attention span guide the conversation. But the spirit of the following reenactment is true to what he (and I) got out of it. What we covered was powerful enough that even years later he can still tell me the pieces of the armor and how they work.

The Full Armor of God
Ephesians 6:10-20 (NIV)

Finally, be strong in the Lord and in his mighty power. Put on the full armor of God, so that you can take your stand against the devil's schemes. For our struggle is not against flesh and blood, but against the rulers, against the authorities, against the powers of this dark world and against the spiritual forces of evil in the heavenly realms. Therefore put on the full armor of God, so that when the day of evil comes, you may be able to stand your ground, and after you have done everything, to stand.

Stand firm then, with the belt of truth buckled around your waist, with the breastplate of righteousness in place, and with your feet fitted with the readiness that comes from the gospel of peace. In addition to all this, take up the shield of faith, with which you can extinguish all the flaming arrows of the evil one. Take the helmet of salvation and the sword of the Spirit, which is the word of God.

And pray in the Spirit on all occasions with all kinds of prayers and requests. With this in mind, be alert and always keep on praying for all the Lord's people. Pray also for me, that whenever I speak, words may be given me so that I will fearlessly make known the mystery of the gospel, for which I am an ambassador in chains. Pray that I may declare it fearlessly, as I should.

Me: So, do you want to put on the armor?
Caden: I guess.

Me: What do you think the belt of truth means?
Caden: Um, being truthful?

Me: Yes. And how would that help you?
Caden: I don't know.

Me: Well, maybe if I could always trust what you say is true it would be easier for us to work together. Like, we're on the same team.
Caden: I guess so.

Me:	What about the breastplate of righteousness? What does that mean and what does it protect?
Caden:	It covers your chest.

Me:	And what important organ is in your chest? *(pointing to his chest)*
Caden:	My heart.

Me:	So, if the breastplate of righteousness covers your chest what do you need to do to protect your heart?
Caden:	I don't know.

Me:	Do you know what righteousness is?
Caden:	No.

Me: It means doing what's right. Do you see how that can protect you? *(no answer)* Every time you choose to do something you know is wrong, it's like the devil won that battle. That's the whole point of the armor—to protect us when we fight the devil. Doing what's right is one way we win. *(more silence)*
What about this one, feet fitted with the readiness that comes from the gospel of peace? Does that make any sense to you?

Caden: Not really.

Me: I think it has to do with sharing Jesus with other people. If we're in a war with the devil we want as many people as possible on our side.

Caden: So, we're building an army and the more people we have the more powerful we are. If I tell people about Jesus, then those people will tell other people and we'll keep growing and we'll be huge.

Me: *(slightly stunned that he grasped and embraced the concept so quickly)* That's right! Maybe we could call it "feet of peace" so it's easier to remember. It's about our feet because it means God doesn't want us to stay where we are and expect people to come to us. We have to go out and look for people. It's like recruiting. How about the shield of faith? The Bible says it will, "extinguish all the flaming arrows of the evil one."

Caden: I'd like to have one of those.

Me: You do. If you have faith that our God is more powerful than the devil it's like a force field of protection. We have to ask God to keep our faith strong.

Caden: Okay.

Me: The next one is the helmet of salvation. What is salvation?

Caden: When you ask Jesus to forgive your sins and come into your heart.

Me: Yep. Have you done that?

Caden: Yes.

Me: Then you've got the helmet. What does that protect?

Caden: My brain. Does that mean I'm smart?

Me: Definitely. The last one is "the sword of the Spirit, which is the word of God." Do you know what that means?

Caden: I know what a sword is.

Me: The word of God is the Bible. This is saying that the Bible is our weapon against the devil.

Caden: How is the Bible a weapon?

Me: The devil hates the words in it. The Bible tells the story of Jesus and in the end Satan loses. But that doesn't keep him from fighting with us and trying to make us miserable. It's his way of getting back at God. We need to remind him that he can't win the war.

Jesus has already beaten him by giving up his life so we can live forever.

Caden: How do I use it as a sword?

Me: We need to read it and find the words that remind us that Jesus is more powerful and memorize those verses. When we are under attack we can say those words and send the devil running away. Like, if the devil is trying to make me afraid to do something that I know I should, I could say, *"I can do all things through Christ who strengthens me."* (Phil. 4:13) Can you see why memorizing Bible verses is so important?

Caden: Yes.

Me: So, let's look back at all the pieces of the armor. Which are offensive and which are defensive? What about the belt of truth?

Caden: Defensive?

Me: I think so too. What about the breastplate of righteousness?

Caden: Defense.

Me: Yes. How about the feet of peace?

Caden: Not sure. You wear it as a part of your armor so it protects you, but maybe it's offensive since you have to go out and get more soldiers.

Me: Good point. Shield of faith?

Caden: Defense.

Me: Helmet of salvation?

Caden: Defense.

Me: Sword of the Spirit?

Caden: Offense.

Me: So, is every part of your body protected?

Caden: *(thinking for a minute)* Not your legs.

Me: True. I wonder if the feet protection is like shin guards. I don't know. But if you have a shield you can probably move that around to cover the part of your body that needs it.

Caden: Not your back.

Me: I never thought of that before. That's really significant. God didn't provide any protection for your back. That means if we run away from the devil we're the most vulnerable.

Caden: So, we can't run.

Me: You're brilliant. Once you take a stand against the enemy you can't wimp out.

Caden: Won't God protect us?

Me: God doesn't force us to do anything. He likes to be asked to be a part of our lives. But he says anything we ask, in his name and for his glory, he'll do for us. (John 14:13-14) And he has angels in his army. They help protect us.

Caden: Really? How do you know they're there?

Me: Jesus said every child has guardian angels. (*"Take heed that you do not despise one of these little ones, for I say to you that in heaven their angels always see the face of My Father who is in heaven."* Matt. 18:10 NKJV)

Caden: Cool. How many angels are there?

Me: I don't know, but the Bible talks about them as armies and legions. So, a bunch. (Matthew 26:53 and Hebrews 12:22) There's a verse about God sending angels to guard us. (Luke 4:10) In the Bible angels aren't pretty and wimpy or like chubby babies with wings, they're mighty warriors. Almost every time they show up they have to tell people not to be afraid, so they must look pretty fierce. The Bible says that a third of the angels chose to be on Satan's side when he left God. That means that two-thirds of the angels are still with God, so we have much more on our team. (Revelation 12) That's about all I can remember about angels.

Caden: That's good.

Me: Does it make you feel better to have armor and an army of angels on your side?

Caden: Yeah.

Me: This chapter in Ephesians ends by telling us to pray. Can I read that part to you again, and then maybe we can pray together?

Caden: Okay.

I have replayed that conversation many times and pondered why it would resonate with my son so much. Several factors stand out—all of which remind me that God meets us where we are. He delights to find a way to teach us in exactly the way that will dig into our hearts and minds and live there forever.

For one thing, this conversion happened after Caden had played a season of flag football. The concepts of offense and defense were fresh for him. He was also at a tipping point in his struggles with ADHD. He was ready to grasp onto anything that would help him take control. Knowing that God had a plan, and that there was an enemy to target, gave him hope and focus.

It was around this point that God revealed the significance of the name we'd given Caden. Before he was born, my husband

and I had disagreed for months about baby names. One evening I was looking through a book of baby names, occasionally mentioning ones I found tolerable—and all receiving negative responses from my husband. Then I suggested Cadell. He came back with, "No, but what about Caden?" I immediately liked it.

Cadell is a Welsh name meaning battler. I wasn't fond of that meaning, but surmised that since we'd just made the name up it didn't have a meaning. God had other thoughts. The more I know my son, the more I see that battling is one of his defining characteristics. We can ignore that and let it grow into a problem or guide it toward something God had planned for him all along.

I used to think fighting was a bad thing. It has definitely been a challenge to parent a child that is wired to fight. But I have also seen this "gift" manifest in positive ways. Caden pushes back against injustices. He doesn't allow others to bully him. He fights for his friends and those that can't fight for themselves. I pray he continues to battle for God's causes for the rest of his life.

I don't tell you this story to say that God will reach your child in exactly the same way. I don't think this armor of God and warfare approach would have ever struck home with me unless I had seen it through my child's eyes.

I would encourage you to pray for the right way to get this idea across to your child: He or she is not alone and there is an enemy to target. We can *do* something to strengthen ourselves. Jesus has a plan for addressing all attacks from the evil one. He had to do it himself. Maybe the story of Jesus's temptation in the wilderness would resonate with your child. Maybe it's a study on angels. Maybe it's simple repetition and reassurance. But it's an important concept for you as a parent and for your child.

Battle Plan

After that conversation with Caden, and on many occasions to follow, we prayed together and put on the armor one piece at a time. We asked God to strengthen the angels that protect us and help us to fight the enemy with a shield of faith and the sword of the spirit.

I would be remiss not to mention that once you make a commitment to stand up to the devil he will probably double his efforts. He is truly evil and will look for every opportunity to scare you back into the frustrated, blame-everyone-else corner you started in. I suggest a plan.

Step 1. Gather your knights. Join with your child and any other friend or family member that is willing, and agree to stay strong in prayer. Encourage each other when it gets difficult. Joined by the strength of the Lord and his hosts of angels you have an army the devil will not waste his effort trying to defeat.

Step 2. Put on the armor with your child. Read it right from the Bible. Or write your own version together. Or use the following prayer.

Dear Jesus,

I will put on the full armor of God so that I am prepared for any attack. I will wear the belt of truth, the breastplate of righteousness and the shoes of the gospel of peace. My shield of faith and helmet of salvation will protect me. I will have the sword of the spirit raised and ready to use. Please help me to be truthful and do what's right. Help me to tell others about you through my words and actions. Thank you for saving me and for forgiving me when I mess up. Strengthen my faith and help me to memorize the words in the Bible so I can use them when things get hard. I also pray for all the other warriors in the army of God. Give us the strength to defeat the enemy and live a life that brings you glory.

Amen.

Pray this together daily for at least a couple weeks, or until you think the list is cemented into your child's memory so they can rely on it when they are feeling under attack. It is good to let a child find their own way of talking to God. Don't keep praying for them indefinitely. Anything done too routinely will start to become meaningless. Do bring it up occasionally. Ask your child to remind you of the pieces of the armor and pray with you so you can feel spiritually stronger.

Step 3. Stock up on ammunition. Find Bible verses that encourage your child and start memorizing. Here's a few ideas to make it fun. You know your child best. The goal is to keep it interesting.

- Make it a game by seeing who can memorize a verse quicker, adults or kids. Take turns picking what verse to memorize.

- If your child is visual or artistic, get them a journal in which to write verses and illustrate them.

- If they are dramatic they could act it out.

- Involve technology.

- If memorization is difficult, find scripture songs and sing along.

Step 4. Strengthen your fortress. You can take all the protective measures we have already mentioned, but if you are welcoming the thief through the back door he will make himself at home. To fortify your home from the inside out, avoid things that Satan would endorse.

What that means for your family is something you'll have to figure out with some prayer and guidance from the Holy Spirit. Fortunately, Philipians 4:8 gives us some rules of thumb. *"Finally, brethren, whatever things are true, whatever things are noble, whatever things are just, whatever things are pure, whatever things are lovely, whatever things are of good report, if there is any virtue and if there is anything praiseworthy—meditate on these things."* (NKJV)

I know, that's setting the bar really high. Ask God how to proceed. It is going to look different for different people. It may require giving up certain TV shows or games. You may need to make a sweep through the house and remove anything that doesn't glorify God all at once. Or, you might decide to change just one thing each week. You could replace violent video games with board games and a weekly game night. Instead of watching questionable movies try volunteering together as a family. Find causes your kids are passionate about.

You don't have to be a fanatic, and it's not your job to convict those outside your home. As much as possible, do this in agreement with your family members. Read the Phil. 4:8 verse above with your family and ask them what things that you have or do that don't fit into the "whatever thing are…" list. Pray that God would lead this charge in his way and without strife.

Step 5. Negotiate Peace. It can't be overstated that our battle is against the devil, not people. With any conflict remind yourself who is trying to kill, steal and destroy peace. Don't let your own words become a tool for the enemy. Pause, pray, and speak life and peace into difficult situations. This will require practice and do-overs. That's ok. We're all just flesh and blood.

Finally, repeat steps one through five as needed. I'm not trying to simplify something as important as spiritual warfare. I'm just a person who likes to have a plan. I can't talk to you about how the devil is looking for opportunities to torment struggling families and not follow it with a discussion on how to fight back. These steps are not a one time assignment or formula. It's an anytime process to refocus on the God of peace.

Wait, Don't Leave Ephesians Six Quite Yet.

God had a bit more to teach me from the sixth chapter of Ephesians. After focusing on the armor of God with my son, I went back and re-read the full chapter. Any final doubts I had about the purpose of spiritual warfare melted away. My desire for peace is God's desire too. We may be battling the evil one, but we need to seek peace with people. The chapter starts with directions for peace in this often contentious human relationship between parent and child.

Ephesians 6:1-4 (NIV)

"Children, obey your parents in the Lord, for this is right. 'Honor

your father and mother'—which is the first commandment with a promise— 'so that it may go well with you and that you may enjoy long life on the earth.'

Fathers, do not exasperate your children; instead, bring them up in the training and instruction of the Lord."

Kids might enjoy the reminder to *"obey your parents,"* a little more if the focus is on the promise of a successful and long life. They might also enjoy knowing that God is giving instruction to their parents as well. *"Do not exasperate your children."*

What does "exasperate" mean to you? There is an important line between encouragement, and unrealistic expectations that set a child up for failure. Finding the right balance to keep frustration and exasperation from destroying my relationship with my child is something that the Holy Spirit has been revealing as I ask for it.

Take the word "no" for example. By the time Caden was eight he had probably heard "no" more often than his own name. As a parent you're supposed to correct your child when he does something unacceptable, right? And we took our parental responsibility seriously to raise our son to be well-behaved. We were also crushing his natural curiosity and lively spirit. He became defeated, anxious and angry, hating his life at such a young age. How do you find the right balance?

That verse in Ephesians gave us some guidance. When we realized how we were *exasperating* him we made a conscious effort to *train* and *instruct* instead. For us that meant taking "no" out of our vocabulary as much as possible. For example, is a no-response really necessary? Maybe it would be ok to say, "Yes, you *can* climb that tree." Sometimes no is necessary, but we replaced negatives with alternatives we could live with. "Instead of climbing the tree why don't you see how many of these rocks you can balance on top of each other. Do you think you can lift that huge one and make it the base of your tower?" Or we found ways for him to understand natural consequences. "Sure, you can play in the mud, but you'll need to do your own load of laundry, and mop the floor if you get it dirty."

This change in vocabulary took a while for us to get used to, but it did slowly make a difference for our son. Removing the constant barrage of negatives, at least at home where we could control it, lifted his self-esteem and improved our relationship. It didn't solve every problem, but it was a tool in our toolbox. One that has been useful even into his teens.

This is the kind of resistance that thwarts the enemy's plans for strife and destruction. When situations are most challenging it helps me to remember whom the battle is against. It is never a battle against my child or any other person. There is a clearly-defined enemy named, *"the spiritual forces of evil."* That is who we fight against. To fight we need strength, and strength comes from prayer. So, we'll ask the question, "Jesus, will you teach me how to pray?"

We may be battling the evil one, but we need to seek peace with people.

Chapter 6

Jesus, Will You Teach Me How To Pray?

I once heard someone comment, "It seems selfish to pray for myself." Perhaps, if you're praying for a million dollars, she was right. I would offer that if you are praying for your own spiritual growth, if you're asking for forgiveness or strength to do what's right, if you're praying for the Holy Spirit to lead you, you are following the example of Christ. In this context, praying for yourself is anything but selfish, it's the best place to start. Let's be honest, we need to get ourselves right with God before we start bringing others into it, right?

Please grab a Bible and read the 17th chapter of John. I'll wait . . . Did you do it? If you tried and didn't get very far, I get it. It's tough reading. In this chapter Jesus was long-winded and hard to follow. But since my goal was to study his words and learn to pray like he did, I put on my thinking cap and dove in. For my own benefit, and maybe yours, I found that his prayer had a method that's surprisingly easy to follow.

> . . . praying for yourself is anything but selfish, it's the best place to start.

With expanding circles, Jesus started with himself, then widened the circle to pray for his disciples, then widened it again to include all believers. I'm pretty sure we can all do that.

Let's take a look at the exact words he prayed in each circle, and think about what that might sound like for each of us as we follow his example.

Circle 1: When Jesus prays for himself he says, *"... Glorify your Son, so that your Son may glorify you—"* John 17:1. (NET) Note the reason he asks for glory—so that God will be glorified. Try putting your own words in a simple prayer and pray it as many times a day as you need to. Let it be the thing that fills the silence when you are unsure what to do or say. Like this:

"Forgive my mistakes, Lord, so that I may glorify you."

"Give me peace, so that I may glorify you."

"Show me the way that would glorify you."

"Increase my faith, so that I may glorify you."

Give it a shot. What does your prayer today, right now, sound like? What is your petition, so that you can glorify God?

Circle 2: When Jesus prays for his disciples he says, *"They belonged to you, and you gave them to me,"* John 17:6 (NET) How like a parent he sounds. I think Jesus wants us to know that he identifies with us as parents. Jesus felt the same love and responsibility for those God placed in his care, as we do for our kids.

> Jesus wants us to know that he identifies with us as parents.

Is your ultimate goal for your son or daughter to thrive without you? That was Jesus's plan for his disciples. His prayer for them gives us a three part plan to equip our kids to do that. Each of our circumstances and children are different. Look for ways to incorporate these three steps in a way that makes sense for your child's comprehension level and at every stage of life. These are not steps you do once and it's done.

Step 1. He teaches them to use the Bible. *"... I have given them the words you have given me." John 17:8* (NET)

If reading and applying the Word of God is a part of our family's (and our own) routine it will show our children we are all still learning. And teaching can be the best way to learn. Can you think of ways your child can teach someone else? Maybe he or she can read the Bible to a little brother or sister, or help out in a younger Sunday school class. Maybe they could plan a weekly Bible study with a friend. These are real-life examples of God's plan for learning as a lifelong process.

Step 2. He prays for their protection and unity with God. *"... Holy Father, keep them safe in your name that you have given me, so that they may be one just as we are one." John 17:11* (NET)

There's not an end date for praying over your children. Plan to do it for the rest of your life. They will always need protection and prayers to strengthen their relationship with God. It doesn't have to be complicated and drawn out, but consider it your assignment as a parent.

Step 3. He lets go. *"Just as you sent me into the world, so I sent them into the world." John 17:18* (NET)

Yikes! This may be the hardest step. But think about it like this; we can practice letting go by finding relatively safe opportunities to give them our trust, and letting go in gradual steps. For most of our children this is about decision making and the ability to learn from failure. If we follow through with this, they will be better prepared and more confident with each new phase of life, until they are, "sent into the world." Jesus exemplified this by giving his disciples trial runs, (Mark 6:7-13) then discussed their experiences with them, correcting and encouraging as needed. As difficult as it is to think about now, there may be a day when your son or daughter has to face life without you. It's not too soon to start giving them the tools they will need to thrive.

If your child has needs that would prevent this kind of independence then the "letting go" is more figurative. *You* will be learning to let go of stress, control and other burdens that you can't carry alone. As you grow in your ability to let go, God will provide opportunities to be, "sent into the world." Whether the lesson is for you or your child, it's about being prepared to be an active participant in the next circle of prayer.

Circle 3: Finally, Jesus prays for all believers. *"I am not praying only on their behalf, but also on behalf of those who believe in me through their testimony,"* John 17:20 (NET) My dear fellow parents, for whom your child's challenges seem all-consuming, Jesus is telling us to look outward. There are others who need prayer and encouragement. Perhaps no one is better-suited than you to extend those gifts.

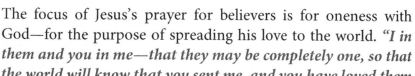
Jesus is telling us to look outward.

The focus of Jesus's prayer for believers is for oneness with God—for the purpose of spreading his love to the world. *"I in them and you in me—that they may be completely one, so that the world will know that you sent me, and you have loved them just as you have loved me."* John 17:23 (NET) Can hear the passion with which Jesus prays for all of us who will come to know him? If we are to use Jesus's words as an example of how to pray, we need to ask him to give us a taste of his deep love for others.

John 17 is a powerful and timeless prayer. With almost every phrase, I can see an appropriate application for my life and family. I personalized the prayer leaving blanks for current circumstances and inserting names. I invite you to join me in prayer for ourselves, our children, and our world.

Dear Father,

Please help me in this area so that I may glorify you:

I ask you to give me the tools and wisdom I need to complete the tasks ahead. I know that you will never leave my side. Help me to feel your presence when I need you most.

I pray for the child(ren) you've given me.

_____ belong(s) to you, but you have trusted me to teach and protect. I will teach your words from the Bible, and share about your sacrifice and salvation. As he/she/they go(es) into the world, please provide protection in the powerful name of Jesus. I know that I will not be able to be there every second, but I trust you.

Help _____ to know you personally and find joy in you. Let his/her/their life point others to your truth and amazing love. This world is broken, so I know there will be challenges my child has to deal with. Let those challenges build strength and faith.

Protect _____ from the evil one. I want him/her/them to know that true love comes from you, so it doesn't matter what the world thinks. We are not part of this world but set apart in the truth of your word. Let me be an example of how to live like Jesus.

Lord, I expand my prayer to other believers—even those that don't know you yet but will someday. I join your desire that we may all be unified in your love. Strengthen all believers to tell, and show, the world how much you love each of us. I lift up families that are struggling like mine. Work through me to offer the encouragement they need. Help us to bond over our shared experiences and goals, to your unending glory.

Amen.

The Prayers of a Child

Since teaching our kids to pray is one of our foremost responsibilities, we need to spend a little time on that topic. Why is it that most children under six are happy to pray out loud? I adore the prayers of a small child. They are so sincere, or at least sincerely imitated from what they've heard. They simply can't do it wrong. Do you ever feel like God can't help but listen to the prayers of a little one? He does, and he listens to your prayers too.

I don't know exactly where I went wrong with my kids, but by the time they were half way through elementary school the only prayers I heard were grudgingly given before a meal or bedtime, and only after a lot of pushing from mom or dad. I don't plan to stop asking them to pray, but maybe a forced prayer isn't what God wants. No matter where you find yourself at this moment, it's not too late to learn more, and teach your children more about prayer.

It may sound like a contradiction, but prayer is both personal and communal. Kids understand better than you might think. Prayer is intensely personal. Jesus said, *"But you, when you pray, go into your room, and when you have shut your door, pray to your Father who is in the secret place; and your Father who sees in secret will reward you openly."* Matthew 6:6 (NKJV) You can take any secret to God. You can pray in your mind or out loud. You can pray alone in your room or during a test at school. You can pray when you're happy or sad. God is with you anytime, anywhere, listening. And if you listen back, he's answering.

Prayer is also meant to be practiced together. There is power in joining with someone in prayer. Our faith gets strengthened and God is delighted with the unity of hearts and minds joined in prayer. This may be a parent and child praying together. It may be a small group of friends taking turns praying aloud. Singing together at church with songs of praise is a form of group prayer. With current technology and social media, hundreds, maybe thousands of people can be praying together within minutes. It's an amazing thought that people all over the world are praying to the same God at the same time. We are truly part of a universal church.

Prayer does not need to be complicated. From Jesus's own words there are a few simple truths that every child should know about prayer.

Kids praise God perfectly.
"Out of the mouth of babes and nursing infants you have perfected praise." Matthew 21:16 (NKJV)

Sometimes, kids understand God better than adults.
"At that time Jesus said, "I praise you, Father, Lord of heaven and earth, because you have hidden these things from the wise and learned, and revealed them to little children. Yes, Father, for this is what you were pleased to do." Matthew 11:25-26 (NIV)

There is power in praying together.
"Again I say to you that if two of you agree on earth concerning anything that they ask, it will be done for them by My Father in heaven. For where two or three are gathered together in My name, I am there in the midst of them." Matthew 18:19-20 (NKJV)

Prayer makes a difference.
"And whatever things you ask in prayer, believing, you will receive." Matthew 21:22 (NKJV)

Prayers can be short and sweet.
"And when you pray, do not use vain repetitions as the heathen do. For they think that they will be heard for their many words." Matthew 6:7 (NKJV)

Get your heart right.
"And whenever you stand praying, if you have anything against anyone, forgive him, that your Father in heaven may also forgive you your trespasses. But if you do not forgive, neither will your Father in heaven forgive your trespasses." Mark 11:25-26 (NKJV)

Never stop teaching and exemplifying these concepts to your child. They may not sink in for a while. But these are seeds that need watering. Keep praying that they will eventually bear fruit.

The summer Caden was 12 he had a breakthrough with worship. He has always resisted doing what the crowd is doing. In Sunday school they would sing songs, but he would be the one kid not doing the hand motions as directed by the leaders. Prayers were to be endured, not joined. At church, during the worship time, he would stay seated when others stood. If I got on his case he would stand but not sing, perfecting his, "I'm bored" face.

You can't force someone to worship God. However, there is something you can do. You can ask God to touch them. No, it didn't occur to me to do that for Caden. I learned it from another 12-year-old boy.

It was at church summer camp—Caden's first multi-night camp without a parent. They had worship and teaching sessions every evening. Ugh. By far that was the worst part of camp for Caden. No running, swimming, climbing, or games, just sit still and try not to get into trouble. Booooring.

A boy named Tate noticed Caden's struggles with worship and had started praying for him. He found a chance to talk with Caden about how worship doesn't have to be boring. He told Caden, "You don't have to bow your head, close your eyes and act like everyone else. You can pray with your eyes open and worship God in your own way. God wants us to be ourselves."

In a text Caden described his experience to us.

"My friend Tate said I could worship God with my eyes open

and it worked. I was praying and worshiping God like I was supposed to, singing and listening. I fell on my knees before God, and I didn't want the service to be over every night after that. I didn't know this was mostly God in me. I didn't know Tate had been praying for me until after that, when he told me."

Caden called us from camp to see if it was ok to get baptized. Of course we would have liked to be there to support him, but that was clearly the right time and place for him. He celebrated his relationship with God, and proclaimed his faith to his peers. The next week his youth pastor asked him to share his story at the youth group. We all agree he experienced a miracle.

There is a footnote to this story because I think it's important to put these emotional highs in the context of everyday life. The week following camp was a rough one for Caden. Fights with his brother ramped up. He was defiant and rude to everyone in the family. So we had a talk.

He expected me to scold him about his behavior. I simply said, when you have a special experience with God, the enemy is going to double his efforts to bring you down. Don't let him win. You are a fighter. Put on your armor. Keep praying and win this battle.

Prayers Without End

I come from a line of prayer-warrior women. My great-grandmother (we called her Minnie-O) was just under five feet tall and about 90 lbs. She was the definition of on-fire-for-God. She could sooner stop breathing than praying. Praises would burst from her mouth mid-conversation, and she would spontaneously jump to her feet and do a little dance out of sheer joy of the Lord.

Her daughter, my grandmother Freeda, spent countless hours on her knees praying over her family. And boy, did she listen to the leading of the Holy Spirit. Whether it was sending me a note and a few dollars just when I needed it most, or knowing that I was expecting a baby before I could tell her, she was in tune with the Lord. I always knew someone was praying on my behalf. Though both of those women have gone to their eternal home, that spirit lives on in my beloved mother who has become my dependable prayer partner.

That heritage is a gift for which I'm more grateful than I can express. But in my lower moments I worry that something is wrong with me that I can't seem to pray for more than ten minutes without getting distracted. I feel guilty, and certain that my kids are doomed because I'm not providing adequate prayer cover for them. I know, that's exactly what the enemy wants me to think.

My consolation comes from the idea that God loves all the different ways we communicate with him. It honors the individualism he created in each of us. Even looking at the three women who have been wonderful examples to me, I see their prayer lives reflect their unique personalities. My prayer life won't look like anyone else's, and it will probably change over the course of my life—hopefully for the better.

> . . . God loves all the different ways we communicate with him.

Bow your head, fold your hands and close your eyes ... Feeling holy? Sorry, I just started thinking about getting the laundry done. I'm sure God loves traditional forms of prayer, but don't you think he enjoys shaking things up too? Can you think of a new way to pray?

I have a friend who visualizes her prayers. Like wisps of smoke or clusters of light each prayer is an offering rising to God. Maybe something like that will help you focus on the prayer instead of the laundry. What else can you think of? I'll start a list of ideas, but brainstorm with your child and add your own unique ways of communicating with The Lord.

1. Sing.
2. Talk to him as you fall asleep. He's ok with you drifting off mid-sentence.
3. Greet him when you wake up.
4. Enjoy his creation—a sunrise/sunset, autumn colors, a breeze that's like a hug.
5. Pray a Bible verse.
6. Tell him when you doubt, get angry, worried or frustrated.
7. Thank him.
8. Ask for forgiveness.
9. Take communion.
10. Join in someone else's prayer.
11. Be still and silent in his presence.
12. List all the ways he is wonderful.

Rock Your Worship

In 1 Thessalonians 5:17 Paul encourages us to pray without ceasing. What a daunting suggestion. How does one pray without ceasing? I believe there are many good answers to this question—none of which have I mastered. From the perspective of teaching the concept to kids I like this thought: We are in our best attitude of prayer when we are in worship. And, since we were created to worship, we are in prayer when we are giving God what we were created to do.

Let's unpack that. In Luke 19:37-40 a multitude of Jesus's followers broke out into spontaneous praise. They must have been getting pretty noisy because some Pharisees told Jesus to shush them. But Jesus answered, *"I tell you, if these were silent, the very stones would cry out."* (ESV) What do you think he means? Beyond the obvious responsibility we have to praise the Lord, there's a fun trail to follow—about the animation of rocks.

I asked Caden, "What do you think about the rocks crying out? Could rocks literally make noise?" He said, "If Jesus told them to, they could." Please give me a moment to be a mom, proud of her son's commendable faith. And I completely agree with him. I would also add that the rock's very existence (animated or not) gives praise to its creator. Ask a geologist or gemologist if we have anything to learn from a rock. Not all humans will acknowledge the rock's creator, but a rock can be pretty special. It can even tell a story just by being what it was created to be.

There are several examples in the Bible of inanimate objects taking on human qualities. Let me share a couple to bring home the point. *"Make a joyful noise to the Lord, all the earth; break forth into joyous song and sing praises! ... Let the sea roar, and all that fills it; the world and those who dwell in it! Let the rivers clap their hands; let the hills sing for joy together."* Psalm 98:4, 7 and 8. (ESV) If you're listening and looking, God's creations are practically deafening in their adoration. And WE are listed right in the middle of that list. Not first or last, but as one of *"those who dwell in"* the earth. Let's follow the example of the seas, the rivers and the hills and worship God as he created us.

When we lift up who we are to the Lord (our talents, traits, gifts, and even faults) for his use and glory, he accepts that as a gift of praise. *"so is my word that goes out from my mouth: It will not return to me empty, but will accomplish what I desire and achieve the purpose for which I sent it. You will go out in joy and be led forth in peace; the mountains and hills will burst into song before you, and all the trees of the field will clap their hands."* Isaiah 55:11-12. (NIV)

To paraphrase; whatever the Lord speaks into existence will accomplish a purpose. You have a purpose! Your child has a purpose! It is no more or less complicated than being who you are for God.

Try asking your child, if you were a rock what could you do to serve God? This might be hard at first, but encourage him to think of buildings, tools, art, and precious stones. What if you were a tree? How could you give yourself to God? What about a river or a mountain? What about yourself? What are your skills and talents? What could God do with all of you? Because that is why you were created and that is your greatest gift of praise. As long as you're giving him you, the praise never ends.

Chapter 7

Revolutionizing Rejection

Jesus is a revolutionary. Over and over he does the unexpected, says the unthinkable and lifts up society's unacceptable. Look at Jesus's Sermon on the Mount. In this speech he turns logic upside down. Here are some examples of his thinking.

> *"Blessed are the poor in spirit ...those who mourn ... the meek ..."* Matthew 5:3-5 (NKJV)

> *"Blessed are you when they revile and persecute you, and say all kinds of evil against you falsely for My sake. Rejoice and be exceedingly glad ..."* Matthew 5:11-12 (NKJV)

> *"You have heard that it was said, 'An eye for an eye and a tooth for a tooth. But I tell you not to resist an evil person. But whoever slaps you on your right cheek, turn the other to him also. If anyone wants to sue you and take away your tunic, let him have your cloak also. And whoever compels you to go one mile, go with him two."* Matthew 5:38-41 (NKJV)

> *"But I say to you, love your enemies, bless those who curse you, do good to those who hate you, and pray for those who spitefully use you and persecute you"* Matthew 5:44 (NKJV)

I love how the Sermon on the Mount ends. It says, *"... the people were astonished ..."* Mat. 7:28. (NKJV)

Of course they were astonished! If you really read his words it's still astonishing. He said to rejoice when you are reviled. He said to do good to those who hate you. What?! From his anger, to his love, to the people he chose as his closest friends, Jesus came to shake things up. He actually says, *"I came to send fire on the earth, and how I wish it were already kindled!"* Luke 12:49

What does this revolution look like for a desperate parent? What is Jesus saying to those of us who have been judged and isolated, or watched our children get rejected? Reading his words above I think it's clear. Jesus wants to wake us up from our tired way of thinking and astonish us. Looking at the unexpected people he called to build his church I think I see his heart. Jesus wants to see our marginalized kids to do amazing things for the Kingdom of God.

In case you hadn't noticed, it wasn't working out so well the way we have been thinking. So why not join the revolution?

> Jesus wants to wake us up from our tired way of thinking and astonish us.

Encouraging the Incorrigible

When my son was in kindergarten he started getting frequent tummy aches. After several weeks and ruling out other factors, we noticed this illness disappeared on the weekends and worsened on the way to school. We asked him if he liked school and he said, "No. I have to sit in time-out all the time."

Fast forward a few years. We were frequently called in to talk to teachers, principals and counselors. Issues ranged from inconsistent grades to bad behavior. There were complaints from other parents about something my son said or did to their child. A teacher once told me that his classmates didn't want to work with him because they were afraid he would get them in trouble. My heart broke for him, but even then, it took me way too long to figure out what was happening. Everyone around him had given up on him being able to do anything right. And he had given up on himself.

We didn't know what to do with these heartbreaks at the moment. But as I turned to the words of Jesus in the Bible, he began to change my despair into a growing excitement. Maybe God had a plan for my son that would astonish everyone who'd ever known him. Passing that conviction on to my son was the best way to change his outlook as well.

Jesus demonstrated that he loves to choose the unexpected. As a student of the scriptures and servant of God, you'd expect Jeesus to be on the same team as the scribes and Pharisees—the highly religious guys. But no, read Matthew 23 for his scathing condemnation of that crew. Instead, Jesus chose to hang out with poor fishermen, despised tax collectors, and scorned sinners. Let's take a quick look at some of the unexpected people Jesus honored.

Matthew Levi was a tax collector. If you think tax collectors are unpopular now, it was much worse in Roman-occupied Israel. The Jewish tax collectors were responsible for taking money from their own people to give to Caesar—the enemy. He would have been considered a traitor, a cheat and a sinner and thus, rejected by his fellow Jews. (Matthew 9: 9-13, Mark 2:14-17, Luke 5:27-32) But, to Matthew Jesus says, *"Follow me."*

John the Baptist was called crazy or demon-possessed by many.

He lived in the wilderness wearing sackcloth, eating weird things, and telling everyone they were sinners. No one wants to hear that. Jesus got seriously upset with those who judged John for his appearance. (Matthew 11:7-19 and Luke 7:24-35) But Jesus saw him through a different lens. In Matthew 11:11 he says, *"... among those born of women there has not risen one greater than John the Baptist ..."* (NKJV)

Simon Peter, known for being impulsive, displayed extremes of passion and violence. He could jump from being courageous to cowardly. But Jesus saw his potential and named him the leader of his future church. *"And I also say to you that you are Peter, and on this rock I will build My church, and the gates of Hades shall not prevail against it. And I will give you the keys of the kingdom of heaven, and whatever you bind on earth will be bound in heaven, and whatever you loose on earth will be loosed in heaven."* Matthew 16:17-19 (NKJV)

The woman at the well was a Samaritan. To the Jews she was from an unclean and despised culture. She was not only a woman, but an adulteress, and currently living with a man who was not her husband. Merely being near her would have scandalized Jesus's peers. But Jesus reached through the walls of convention, treated her with respect and changed her life. (John 4:1-42)

Have you watched your child experience rejection? Have you been scorned because of the way you handle your kid? It's a common story. Jesus himself knew rejection. In Mark 9:12 he says of himself, *"...concerning the Son of Man, that He must suffer many things and be treated with contempt..."* (NKJV) However, if you were looking for Jesus to join your pity party, you're going to be disappointed.

He agreed, it's a tough world out there. He experienced hate thousands of years ago, and it's not much different today. Good news: Our joy and peace don't come from the world anyway. It comes from Jesus. *"These things I have spoken to you, that in Me you may have peace. In the world you will have tribulation; but be of good cheer, I have overcome the world."* John 16:33 (NKJV)

> . . . if you were looking for Jesus to join your pity party, you're going to be disappointed.

Hey, I'm Calling You. Yes, YOU.

Jesus is relentless in his faith in us. No matter how much we mess up, he still trusts us to carry out his mission. Jesus chooses flawed people because it brings greater glory to God. When he works through us, in spite of ourselves, there's no way we can take the credit for ourselves. He's an expert at seeing the potential in things that others ignore or dismiss.

Another parable He put forth to them, saying: "The kingdom of heaven is like a mustard seed, which a man took and sowed in his field, which indeed is the least of all the seeds; but when it is grown it is greater than the herbs and becomes a tree, so that the birds of the air come and nest in its branches." Matthew 13:31-32 (NKJV)

Jesus will never give up pursuing us. He already sacrificed his life for us. And, while he never forces us to choose his way, he is always asking. The Parable of the Lost Sheep reminds us how he will focus on those that need him most.

"What do you think? If a man has a hundred sheep, and one of them goes astray, does he not leave the ninety-nine and go to

the mountains to seek the one that is straying? And if he should find it, assuredly, I say to you, he rejoices more over that sheep than over the ninety-nine that did not go astray. Even so it is not the will of your Father who is in heaven that one of these little ones should perish. Matthew 18:12-14 (NKJV)

> Jesus is relentless in his faith in us.

When you give your life to Jesus he sees you as perfect. We need to tell our children they are perfect through Jesus. They have been chosen for a special mission. Meditate on these words of Jesus, for yourself and for your child.

> *"Therefore you shall be perfect, just as your Father in heaven is perfect."* Matthew 5:48 (NKJV)

> *"You are the light of the world. A city that is set on a hill cannot be hidden. Nor do they light a lamp and put it under a basket, but on a lampstand, and it gives light to all who are in the house. Let your light so shine before men, that they may see your good works and glorify your Father in heaven."* Matthew 5:14-16 (NKJV)

> *"You did not choose Me, but I chose you and appointed you that you should go and bear fruit, and that your fruit should remain, that whatever you ask the Father in My name He may give you."* John 15:16 (NKJV)

Let me share a couple stories of people who have demonstrated Jesus-like faith in my child. These heroes have given me an example of how to live Jesus's words with everyday deeds. As a parent who has tried "everything" to help my child, I consider the results of their actions nothing short of miraculous.

A neighbor had to send my son home from their house because he wasn't following her rules. She told him, "I explained the rules of our house and I'm sorry you weren't able to follow them. Our rules are important to our family so you'll have to leave." But she didn't leave it at that. She showed faith in him by adding, "But, I know you can do better. I hope you'll come back on a different day and try again."

She could have blamed me for his behavior. She could have forbidden her children to play with him. Instead, she called me to explain what happened and assured me they cared about him. My son asked me if he could apologize. Which he did, and was received with a hug. The next time he was invited to their house he tried harder to do the right thing. By extending forgiveness *and* high expectations to Caden, that mother demonstrated Jesus's love to our whole family.

Sports have been both a blessing and a curse for Caden. He's naturally active, athletic, competitive, determined and practically impervious to pain. He's also known to be stubborn, defiant, argumentative, and easily distracted. Over the years we have tried just about every sport in search of a good fit. At the beginning of fourth grade he got it in his head that he wanted to play soccer—again. He hadn't played since first grade. I wondered if he'd missed too much over the last few years to just jump back in. Not only did he insist on playing soccer, he had his heart set on being a goalkeeper.

I tried to explain that he would need to practice hard, learn as much as he could and be willing to play whatever position the coach put him in. He pestered the coach and at the second game of the season the coach let Caden start as goalie. It was a disaster. He was doing everything his own way, ignoring or arguing with the coach and his teammates. I lost count of the goals scored on him until he was pulled out at half time. I understood why, but was sorry to see him fail at what he wanted so badly.

At the beginning of the next game I watched the coach pull Caden aside and talk to him for several minutes. Then, my husband and I watched in stunned surprise as Caden pulled on the goalkeeper jersey and walked over to take his place in front of the goal.

I still don't know what the coach said or why he decided to give Caden another chance, but the results were amazing. He played like part of a team. For several seasons Caden stayed with that team as their main goalkeeper. The coach's display of grace motivated my son in a way that I don't think anything else could.

I'm incredibly grateful for the lessons I have learned from these people. As I strive to live more like them, I remember that the ultimate example is Jesus. He always sees the maximum potential and encourages us to amaze the doubters.

Jesus Never Promised it Would be Easy

This parenting gig may not look exactly how you pictured it. I can say it has been fun, frustrating, amazing, heartbreaking, educational, and incredibly rewarding. But it has definitely not been easy. When Jesus calls, he promises to equip you for the task. He promises he'll never leave you. He never said there won't be challenges. He practically guarantees there will.

"Enter by the narrow gate; for wide is the gate and broad is the way that leads to destruction, and there are many who go in by

it. Because narrow is the gate and difficult is the way which leads to life, and there are few who find it." Matthew 7:13-14 (NKJV)

Jesus is asking for a revolution of your mindset. James, the brother of Jesus, summarizes this for us. *"Consider it pure joy, my brothers and sisters, whenever you face trials of many kinds, because you know that the testing of your faith produces perseverance. Let perseverance finish its work so that you may be mature and complete, not lacking anything.* James 1:2-4 (NIV)

Jesus is asking for a revolution of your mindset.

So, let's set aside our preconceived ideas about what kids are supposed to be like, and how parenting is supposed to work. Let's be open to a new and better (not necessarily easier) way—the Jesus way.

Need something more specific? Let James finish his thought. *"If any of you lacks wisdom, you should ask God, who gives generously to all without finding fault, and it will be given to you. But when you ask, you must believe and not doubt, because the one who doubts is like a wave of the sea, blown and tossed by the wind. That person should not expect to receive anything from the Lord. Such a person is double-minded and unstable in all they do."* James 1:5-8 (NIV)

Can it be so simple? All we have to do is ask? Jesus says yes. He even puts it in terms that we parents can relate to. Of course, we want to give the best of everything to our children. However, the best isn't always what they think they want. And we can't always explain why—at least not in a way that they can fully understand. Think of yourself as God's child. We want our kids to trust us. God is asking the same of you.

"Ask, and it will be given to you; seek, and you will find; knock, and it will be opened to you. For everyone who asks receives, and he who seeks finds, and to him who knocks it will be opened. Or what man is there among you who, if his son asks for bread, will give him a stone? Or if he asks for a fish, will he give him a serpent? If you then, being evil, know how to give good gifts to your children, how much more will your Father who is in heaven give good things to those who ask Him! Therefore, whatever you want men to do to you, do also to them, for this is the Law and the Prophets." Matthew 7:7-12 (NKJV)

The following parable is perfect for parents of kids with struggles. It reminds me that some things are going to require extra work. You don't give up just because the devil tries to make life harder. Jesus thinks the effort is worthwhile, and so do I.

Jesus told them another parable: "The kingdom of heaven is like a man who sowed good seed in his field. But while everyone was sleeping, his enemy came and sowed weeds among the wheat, and went away. When the wheat sprouted and formed heads, then the weeds also appeared.

"The owner's servants came to him and said, 'Sir, didn't you sow good seed in your field? Where then did the weeds come from?'

"'An enemy did this,' he replied.

"The servants asked him, 'Do you want us to go and pull them up?'

"'No,' he answered, 'because while you are pulling the weeds, you may uproot the wheat with them. Let both grow together until the harvest. At that time I will tell the harvesters: First collect the weeds and tie them in bundles to be burned; then gather the wheat and bring it into my barn.'" Matthew 13:24-30 (NIV)

You can continue reading through verse 43 for Jesus's full explanation of the parable, but here's the headline: The task at hand may require even more than just hard work. Financial, personal, or physical sacrifices may be asked of you and your family. But Jesus asks us to keep our perspectives in order. Focus on the eternal treasure.

> We want our kids to trust us. God is asking the same of you.

A Change of Perspective.

Have you ever wished you could read minds? The impulsivity of ADHD sort of grants that wish for me. My son usually says the first thing that pops into his head. Without the filter that most of us employ, much of what he says, unfortunately, tends to be disrespectful or inappropriate. This was becoming a huge source of strife in our family when Jesus showed me a different point of view.

Read the parable of the two sons (Matthew 21:28-32 NKJV) and consider the question Jesus posed to the religious leaders.

"But what do you think? A man had two sons, and he came to the first and said, 'Son, go, work today in my vineyard.' He answered and said, 'I will not,' but afterward he regretted it and went. Then he came to the second and said likewise. And he answered and said, 'I will, sir,' but he did not go. Which of the two did the will of his father?" They said to Him, "The first."

What do you think? Until recently my answer would have been neither. The first son disrespected his father. That's not what God wants from us, is it? The second son said what his father wanted to hear, but didn't follow through. That's definitely not

God's will either. Jesus agrees with their answer, the first son. He even goes on to explain it, but I didn't really understand it until firsthand experience with my son enlightened me. First read Jesus's response.

Jesus said to them, "Assuredly, I say to you that tax collectors and harlots enter the kingdom of God before you. For John came to you in the way of righteousness, and you did not believe him; but tax collectors and harlots believed him; and when you saw it, you did not afterward relent and believe him."

Here's how I interpret what he's saying. Jesus compares those who want to know him but don't know how to say the right words, to those that say the right words but have no intention of doing the right thing. God showed me that Caden was like the first son. He has it in his heart to do what was right, but he needs time and space to put it into action.

We have found that he responds better when we trust him to do the right thing, than to our threats and expectation that he'll do the wrong thing. When you think about it, who wouldn't? In this parable Jesus shows his soft spot for those who struggle to do what everyone expects. He has faith in them. How could I do less for my own son?

One morning as we were getting ready for church, I asked my son to button up his shirt. He said, "No. I like it like this." I looked at the old, stained t-shirt he was wearing under his nice shirt, and weighed it against the argument it would take to get the shirt buttoned. Difficult as it was for me, I shut my mouth and we loaded into the car.

About half way to church, he said, "Mom, does this look good?" I turned to see he had every button done—all the way to his chin. I told him he looked great. Then, I told him the parable of the two sons. He immediately said, "Hey, that's just like me. I don't like to say what people want me to say." I am grateful for this parable because it helped me understand him better, and to trust him to do what's right. It gives me patience when his words are defiant. I guarantee I'll need reminders in the coming years, but when I read this parable it feels like Jesus told it just for me because he knew I'd need it to connect with my son.

We have a list of traits we call Caden's superpowers. Some might consider them flaws, but we are flipping that perspective. Here are some examples. His distractibility means he can hear everything—even when multiple conversations and noises fill a room. This is like super-sonic hearing. The past and future may be abstractions to him, but his ability to be fully in the present is exactly what God asks us to do. He is way ahead of most of us in that respect. His hyperactivity means he'd usually rather have fun outdoors than vegetate in front of a screen. His defiance gives him the power to stand up for what's right.

You get the idea. Whatever is frustrating you could be a gift, if you examine it from a different perspective. Revolutionize expectations of failure. Ask God to show you how your child's traits can be directed toward success. Follow the example of Jesus to encourage the incorrigible, raise up the marginalized, and cheer on the defeated.

Chapter 8

Peace That Passes Understanding

Another mother with two boys, picked up me and my two boys for a Saturday afternoon movie. We filed into the crowded theatre and found seats for the two younger kids right behind us moms, while we let the older boys sit on their own. The other family went to buy some snacks while my family held the seats. I had told my boys in advance that I would not be buying concessions. I'm cheap. They could use their own money or just wait until we got home to snack. But seeing his friend with popcorn and a soda was too much for Caden. He began to whine, then beg, then throw a fit. The previews were starting, the lights dimming, and heads were turning in our direction. I slipped from my seat to go get him some water.

When I got back the theatre was dark and quiet. The feature had begun. I found my seat and turned to hand the cup to Caden. He was still fuming and blaming me for making his life miserable. He snatched the cup from me, not realizing there wasn't a lid, and soaked himself. The freak out leveled up.

"Mom! My shorts are all wet! Look what you did!" As quietly as possible I asked if he wanted to leave. He just glared at me. Someone nearby shushed us, so I turned around and sat down. Then he started kicking my seat. Not just tapping it, but stomping on the back of my chair with one foot, then both, with all his strength.

I turned and told him to knock it off. He said, "No. This is your fault." A man behind us said, "You need to make that kid be quiet." I stood up, reached over and tried to physically lift Caden to take him out of the theatre, but he wedged himself into the chair. There was no budging him. I sat back down. The kicking continued.

I looked at my friend and together we turned around, each of us grabbing an arm and we put our backs into it. Nothing. He was a determined nine-year-old, not a toddler. At this point I noticed that he had tears running down his cheeks. And I knew. I knew he didn't want to be doing this. He was embarrassed. He was in pain. He was grasping for control and failing. He didn't know how to stop it.

I let go and just looked at him, aching for him and not knowing what to do. The man from behind made another comment. My friend told him, "Relax, it's a kid's movie. Kids are noisy." Caden snapped out of it, vaulted out of his seat, scrambled over mine, and ran out of the theatre.

I darted after him, but by the time I reached the lobby he was nowhere in sight. I stood still, scanning the area. There. I just caught a glimpse of him as he ran out of the building. Then he was running across the parking lot. Where in the world was he going? How was I going to catch him? I didn't have a car, couldn't wait for my friend to come out, didn't want to ruin the movie for the other three kids, and my husband was out of town. Dear Lord, protect him.

Taking a deep breath I ran out after him. He was so far ahead of me. Within a minute I was winded, but he kept running. Finding a slow jog I could maintain, I managed to at least keep him in sight. I watched him approach a busy intersection and started to panic. To my relief he slowed, pushed the crosswalk button and waited for the light to change. Thank God!

He crossed the street and resumed his pace. How long could he keep running? How long could I? After a few more lights he slowed. Then he turned and saw me about a block behind. He picked up his pace again, but continued to stop and safely cross every street. Eventually he settled into a walk and I gained on him.

About a mile from the theatre we were walking side by side. Half a mile later I broke the silence. "You have a pretty good sense of direction. Do you think you can get us home from here?" He nodded and said, "I think we need to turn right at the next light." I said, "Lead the way. I trust you. Let me know if you want help."

I texted my friend to let her know we wouldn't be coming back and asked her to drop off my other son after the show. Caden navigated our four-mile walk home perfectly. We didn't talk about the incident. Rehashing it didn't seem useful. The exercise calmed him and I gradually let my stress slip away. For the rest of the walk, for the rest of the day, we embraced peace.

Peace, Be Still!

On the same day, when evening had come, He said to them, "Let us cross over to the other side." Now when they had left the multitude, they took Him along in the boat as He was. And other little boats were also with Him. And a great windstorm arose, and the waves beat into the boat, so that it was already filling. But He was in the stern, asleep on a pillow. And they awoke Him and said to Him, "Teacher, do You not care that we are perishing?"

Then He arose and rebuked the wind, and said to the sea, "Peace, be still!" And the wind ceased and there was a great calm. But He said to them, "Why are you so fearful? How is it that you have no faith?" And they feared exceedingly, and said to one another, "Who can this be, that even the wind and the sea obey Him!" Mark 4:35-41 (NKJV)

Peace in the middle of a storm may seem impossible to you right now. Are you battered by winds and rain? Are you frantically bailing water from your sinking ship, only to have it swamped by the next wave? Have you felt that Jesus must not care since he's not doing anything to save you?

> Are you asking Jesus to intervene, but not letting him?

I find it interesting that with three words, *"Peace, be still!"* Jesus instantly calmed all external elements, but the storm continued to rage in the disciples' hearts and minds. *After* the storm was stilled, it says, *"they feared exceedingly."* Why? He did what they asked of him. Were they so uncomfortable with Jesus's miraculous solution they might have been happier to perish in their problem? Are you asking Jesus to intervene, but not letting him?

Here's the real lesson for me: Jesus doesn't control me, or you, or anyone else. He offers peace, but he doesn't force us to accept it. From our internal storms to the gales that whip around us let's face the challenges to peace in our families. Let's discern what we can and cannot control. Let's look to Jesus for true internal peace, and find faith in the midst of fear.

Don't Play the Blame Game

"I must have done something wrong when I was pregnant ..." "If only I'd breast-fed for a few more months ..." "We let him watch too much TV ... eat too much sugar ... play with the wrong kids

..." "I should have prayed more ... punished differently ... been more forgiving ..."

This is what our internal storms can sound like. *But what if it's true?* Even if any self-chastisement is appropriate, is it productive? Give that a moment of honest reflection. If there is a nagging thought that your current struggles are because of some past failure, ask this question: Do I need to address that issue in order to be a better parent going forward? Focus on the forward. Refuse to let the past do anything but inspire improvement.

Remember the story of the man with the epileptic son? After watching the child in an episode Jesus asked the father, *"How long has this been happening to him?"* The father answered, *"Since he was very young."* Mark 9:21. (ERV) This family had been in turmoil for as long as they could remember.

If you were to observe my son at his most out of control moments and ask me, "How long has he been like this?" I would think back. As soon as Caden was old enough to run I remember saying to my husband, "It's like he has an uncontrollable urge to just go. He's not thinking about whether he'll be able to find us when he stops."

Maybe it was even farther back than that. He was not a baby that wanted to be snuggled. He has always either been in motion or sleeping like a rock. Is this a fault? Do I need to blame myself or someone else for this? No. This is who my child is. And if I think I love him, it's nothing compared to God's unlimited and unconditional love. So, I will thank the Lord for my son. I will pray for wisdom on how to raise him to work with his nature so God can fully use him for good.

> Refuse to let the past do anything but inspire improvement.

If we're not blaming ourselves we're often pointing fingers at others. Have you said, "My spouse just makes things worse..." "This teacher isn't doing her job..." "Nobody understands what we're going through..."

In a way, blaming everyone else is even worse than blaming yourself. Essentially, you may be alienating your best resources. It is to your (and your child's) benefit to try to find a way to work with everyone in his or her life. However, this is the point where we move away from what we can control. We can, and should, pray for those around us. But Jesus doesn't force anyone to do the right thing.

Yes, some people can be incredibly difficult! Maybe it is someone in your family, or someone at school, or a neighbor, or maybe even someone at church that is causing strife and pain for you or your child. So, what do you do about these storm-starters? You're probably not going to like the answer. I didn't.

If limiting exposure to a negative person is not an option, you can 1. pray and 2. change yourself. Never underestimate what both of those things can accomplish. But, that may be all you can actually *do*. You simply can't make someone else change.

Maybe you're directing the blame at God. Have you thought, "God, how could you do this to me..." "Why do you allow so much pain in my life... for my child... in the world?" Have you questioned God's existence, or at least his goodness?

You are not alone. Many have turned away from God because of pain, suffering, or unanswered prayer. It's human. But God is not human. He can handle our anger and doubt. In fact, I think he welcomes it. Telling God you hate him is still talking to him. Doubting him means you had hope in him to begin with—or you wouldn't feel so disappointed. Letting God know how you feel is honest and real.

When we pour out our frustrations on him, he accepts them with limitless understanding. If we allow him to share our pain, and allow ourselves to listen, he has a response. He asks you to have faith that he loves you. He wants you to believe that he will use your situation for good.

The enemy will use fear and doubt to punch holes in my boat. I know how to guard myself with the shield of faith, and all the other pieces of the armor of God. Still, there are going to be times I take my eyes off Jesus and panic at the storm around me.

It has taken me ages to write this little book because of self-doubt. I would work on it a little and then make a bunch of excuses to avoid getting back to it. I knew the words of Jesus were true, but I wasn't able to consistently put them into practice. Sometimes I felt completely unworthy to write another word. It is only because of the Lord's forgiveness, and these beautiful words, that I could shake off the guilt to step where he was leading me.

"So now there is no condemnation for those who belong to Christ Jesus." Romans 8:1 (TLB)

Here's the thing: Jesus has as much love and forgiveness and FAITH IN ME as he does my child. I can keep failing and he will keep expecting the best from me. The bigger challenge may be to believe in myself.

> I can keep failing and he will keep expecting the best from me.

I didn't start writing again because I suddenly got my act together and felt worthy. I took a leap of faith. I trusted that if I started following Jesus's examples, he would start to transform me into the type of parent he would be. Jesus said, *"A disciple is not above his teacher, but everyone who is perfectly trained will be like his teacher."* Luke 6:40. (CSB) I can't say mission accomplished yet, but I am better each time I shake off fear and step into faith. With each decision I make to see myself through Jesus's eyes, a habit begins to develop, and it's a little easier next time.

Dear fellow parent in the boat, Jesus has FAITH IN YOU too. You have to believe that. You must act on that knowledge even if you don't feel it. Your leap of faith may be a daily decision to forgive yesterday's mistakes and follow Jesus with each step forward. It is essential because you will need to model your capacity to grow, and be a living example of Jesus's faith in us to your kids. Don't panic. He never stops offering guidance and the Bible is full of pep talks. Revisit the encouraging verses in the previous chapter to get you started.

Illusive Peace

I can relate to the disciples in the storm—more afraid of God's solution than the problem. Nobody wants to step into the uncomfortable, the unknown. My boys were four and eight the first time I had what would become a recurring nightmare. It sounds weird to say, but I now believe that God gave me that nightmare. Because it was too hard for me to face and process what the dream might mean, I pushed it away for years. I failed to see the comfort and guidance God was trying to give. But, with the perspective of time, the meaning is crystal clear.

> *A strong breeze fills my nose with the briny-fishy smell of the ocean, and whips my hair around my face. I push*

away the salt-hardened strands and refocus my attention on the two little boys in front of me. Ethan, my older son, is focused on the tricky work of adding a tower to his sandcastle. Caden, the younger one, mimics his brother's actions, adding his own inspiration. He scoops sand into a yellow bucket with a blue spade. He dumps the sand into a pile, then joyfully flattens the mound with wide-spread fingers.

"Caden! You're going to mess it up.!" Ethan says, scowling at his brother. Caden jumps up and runs around the perimeter of the carefully crafted moat spraying sand in his wake.

"Here," I say, handing the bucket to Caden. "Go fill this with water." He takes the bucket and bounds toward the surf. I follow him with my eyes. Another gust tangles my hair around my face. Holding my hair back with one hand and improvising a visor with the other I see Caden farther away than I expect. The water had been just a few yards away. Now, it looks four times the distance.

I look past my child running across the flat and glistening sand, past the receding shoreline, and toward the horizon. Something looks wrong, but I can't make sense of it. I hear shouts. My periphery registers people running away from the beach. About the same time my mind connects what's happening I hear the word that defines it.

"Tsunami!" Someone yells as they run by. I bolt up and scream Caden's name as I sprint toward him. Panic surrounds me like glue, reducing my speed to slow

motion. Tears of frustration choke my shouts. I am try-
ing to run faster, to call louder, but it doesn't seem to be
working. Mentally, I beg him to hear me and turn
around. Finally I reach him, scoop him up, and curve
back around without slowing.

Ethan stands by his castle, wide-eyed and waiting. My
mind calculates our limited options. The boy in my
arms is heavy. I cannot carry them both. I shift Caden
to one side and reach my other hand out to Ethan. We
lock hands and keep running, but I know we won't be
fast enough. The exertion already has me trembling
and I hear the rush of blood pounding in my ears. No,
wait. It's the ground that's shaking. And the roar is
coming from the ocean behind us.

Ahead, I see a small tree. Its windswept branches don't
instill much confidence, but it is stout with low limbs. I
think we can quickly climb up about ten feet, maybe
more. I decide. Pushing Ethan ahead I yell for him to
climb the tree. I lift Caden onto a thick branch then
hoist myself after him. We scramble up as far as we can
and cling to each other around the center trunk.

From my perch I see the monstrous wall of water
approaching. The certainty that we will be swallowed
by its jaws is an unavoidable truth. I look at my sons. I
don't know if any of us will survive this, but I can't help
both of them. I have to choose. How can I possibly
choose? I can't. But if I try to save them both, we will all
drown. I have seconds to process this. I choose.

"Ethan," I shout over the roaring. He looks into my eyes

and I grab his face with my hand. "You are a strong swimmer. You will swim. You will live. And I will find you." I can't read his expression. Does he feel betrayed? I don't have time to give that more than a fleeting thought. I wrap both of my arms around Caden and brace for the impact. Deafening noise and shearing wind overwhelm every sense. Then, nothing.

I woke with my heart racing and tears in my eyes. Over the next few years the same dream resurfaced three or four times. I didn't tell anyone about it. I didn't talk to God about it, or try to analyze it. I didn't even want to think about it. In 2012 ads started running for the movie *The Impossible,* a true story about a family caught up in a tsunami. Just watching the movie trailer once left me sobbing. Any time I saw the ad come up I changed the channel or left the room.

I honestly didn't give the dream my full attention for over a dozen years. A friend asked me if I had any fears. I thought about the dream. By this point my boys were 16 and 20. Surely enough time had passed that I should be able to talk about it. I decided to share. However, before I could finish my very abbreviated version of the dream I was in tears. Clearly, I still needed to process something. Long overdue, I prayed about it and faced my fear.

Through the lense of time it wasn't so difficult to understand the dream. I had one child that had monopolized my time and efforts. And, as much as I tried not to, my other child was sometimes neglected.

One of the most difficult things that the devil has stirred up in our family is division between my sons. For a long time I thought it was just normal sibling rivalry. But by the time Ethan reached his teenage years I had to face the fact that a deep bitterness was festering. Years of his brother pestering, manipulating, and demanding attention had taken its toll.

Yes, I feel responsible and often wonder what we should have done differently. We explored a number of different approaches—from high intervention to letting them work it out for themselves. We tried keeping them as separated as possible to non-optional family fun. We tried logical and emotional appeals to each of them to try to get along. I begged God to soften their hearts for each other. Nothing really worked. They fought, criticized, or avoided each other. No matter how much we bailed water and patched leaks, we always had that swamp in the bottom of our boat.

God tried to help me by sending me a dream. It wasn't to scare me. It was a warning to pray about the coming storm. God knew the turmoil that was going to break my heart. He wanted to walk alongside us and help me listen to his guidance. Regrettably, I shut him out when I should have leaned into him for comfort. That doesn't mean he left us.

God uses all things for good—even when I mess up. I feel guilty for not protecting Ethan better, for not being involved enough. But he has grown up to be an independent and self-motivated young man, standing at the threshold of medical school. While they're not best friends (yet) he almost seems to like his brother—now that they're not living in the same house. Sometimes they text each other. And recently, they actually went out together to grab a milkshake. These are the things that will warm a mother's heart.

Peace Revealed

When I don't hear Jesus offering a solution, and don't see him bailing water beside me, it's easy to think he doesn't care. That's not how Jesus works, though. When I am tempted to think he's not with me I can picture him getting just as frustrated with me as he did his disciples in the boat, saying, *"Why are you so fearful? How is it that you have no faith?"*

When everything that I can do has been done, all that's left is faith. This is the definition of peace that passes understanding— it doesn't have to make sense to exist. The peace Jesus offers doesn't just come when everything is going right. His peace is available in the darkest pit and wildest storm. It seems a no-brainer to just accept it. Why do we have so much trouble doing that?

It's hard to discern the difference between the storm raging within us and the storm around us. Even if Jesus calmed your external storm, there is no peace until your internal one is still. Releasing blame of any kind is essential for peace. How in the world do you do that? Jesus has an answer: Shift the focus from blame to how God can be glorified through adversity. Jesus was doing just that in this next story found in John 9:1-7. (NKJV)

Now as Jesus passed by, He saw a man who was blind from birth. And His disciples asked Him, saying, "Rabbi, who sinned, this man or his parents, that he was born blind?" Jesus answered, "Neither this man nor his parents sinned, but that the works of God should be revealed in him. I must work the works of Him who sent Me while it is day; the night is coming when no one can work. As long as I am in the world, I am the light of the world." When He had said these things, He spat on the ground and made clay with the saliva; and He anointed the eyes of the blind man with the clay. And He said to him, "Go, wash in the pool of Siloam" (which is translated, Sent). So he went and washed, and came back seeing.

> Shift the focus from blame to how God can be glorified through adversity.

Relinquishing blame shifts your focus away from the past. Relinquishing worry shifts it away from the future. Where does that leave you? Exactly where Jesus wants you.

"But seek first his kingdom and his righteousness, and all these things shall be yours as well. Therefore do not be anxious about tomorrow, for tomorrow will be anxious for itself. Let the day's own trouble be sufficient for the day." Matthew 6:33-34 (RSV)

Can you imagine the gaping hole it would leave in our minds if we let go of worry and overthinking? How do we fill the void? Jesus has advice for that as well. Read the first sentence of that last passage again.

"All these things" refers to what we think we want. Jesus is not saying that our wants are bad. In fact, our desires are often very good—even planted by God. He is just reminding us to look at our priorities. It's a reality check about what we can control and who is *really* in control. The better way is to seek God first.

All those ideals, plans and dreams you have—can you give them to God? If our desires align with God's then he'll bring them about in the perfect time and way. No amount of stress and striving can make our desires a reality better than what God has planned.

The words of Paul seem an appropriate reiteration. He says, *"Be anxious for nothing, but in everything, by prayer and supplication, with thanksgiving, let your requests be made known to God; and the peace of God, which surpasses all understanding, will guard your hearts and minds through Christ Jesus.* Philippians 4:6-7. (NKJV) This verse is my prayer for you, dear friend. And, if you don't mind me joining in, for me too.

Do you remember the first words of Jesus we examined in this book? As you read it again let his concern wash over you. Claim the promise he offers.

"Come to Me, all you who labor and are heavy laden, and I will give you rest. Take My yoke upon you and learn from Me, for I am gentle and lowly in heart, and you will find rest for your souls. For My yoke is easy and My burden is light." Mat. 11:28-30 (NKJV)

Since starting this book, the weight of your situation may not have changed an ounce. But I pray you are better equipped for the journey. The burden is meant to be shared with Jesus. The view of yourself, your child, the people around you, and the road ahead, is meant to be seen through Jesus's eyes. Let these words of our savior lighten your step, and the next, and the next.

Jesus Promised

Middle school loomed like a shadowy threat. I tried to stay optimistic. After all, fifth grade had gone pretty well. A great teacher, along with some social and athletic successes combined to put Caden on the best possible path.

But I knew sixth grade would bring a new level of expectations. Multiple teachers, classes, and assignments, added homework, and a tight schedule would require organizational skills I wasn't sure my son could live up to. And that doesn't even touch on the social minefield that is middle school.

Parent night was right after the first day of school. I hadn't even had a chance to ask Caden how his day had gone before joining the crowd of other parents experiencing their child's schedule in fast forward. As I moved from class to class each teacher outlined his or her plans for the year. I felt despair begin to weigh me down. A barrage of questions filled my mind. How is he going to handle this? The workload will be overwhelming. We can't expect any of these teachers to help him, they each have over a hundred students. His handwriting is slow and barely legible. He can't take notes like they're asking. By evening he's burned out trying to control himself. When is he going to get all this homework done?

I fought back the sting of tears and the lump in my throat. Once home I found my son. With trepidation asked him how he liked his first day in middle school. His eyes lit up and he said, "It was really great."

He spoke enthusiastically about his teachers. He said he liked moving from class to class instead of being in the same room all day. He loved having a locker. He looked forward to science experiments and gym class. He was going to do great in speech and drama—because he's not afraid to talk in front of other people. Oh, and that teacher gave them an assignment to tell the class all about themselves, which just happens to be his favorite subject.

He gushed about school for some time. Then I (with little faith) asked him if he could handle having more homework than he was used to. He (with much faith) said, "No problem. I'm going to be organized and get great grades."

Then, he asked us to give him a chance to be completely in charge of his own homework: don't ask him about it, don't insist on looking it over, don't check his organizer. (Yikes! Give him our total faith?) Under the condition that he stay after school every day to get his homework done before coming home, and that no teachers contacted us with concerns, we agreed—situation to be reviewed after the first quarter.

We honored our side of the agreement and gave him the independence and trust he requested. It was so, so difficult to step aside. What kind of parents don't check on their kids' school work? Ones that don't care, right? But you know what? Life got easier. No nagging, no arguing, no punishing. And he owned it. He organized his room and backpack. He attended the after school program where kids can do their homework with a teacher. He monitored his own grades online, frequently showing us his As and Bs. It was wonderful. Of course, a little part of me was skeptical. Could this possibly continue?

Parent-teacher conferences gave me the answers I needed. Every single teacher I visited had a similar story. Caden was doing great. He was funny, creative, and smart. There had been a time or two when he misbehaved, but nothing extreme. When he was corrected, he was respectful, and he made an effort to do better. He missed an occasional assignment, but his grades were good. Sometimes he was fidgety, but he tried not to bother the kids around him. Not one teacher had concerns, suggested changes, or asked for our involvement.

If you're a parent that knows the dread of parent-teacher conferences you can imagine the cloud I floated home on. I couldn't wait to tell Caden about all the good reviews, and how proud I was. To my shame, it took me about a day to remember to thank God for his work in my son's life.

Of course it was God at work. I can't credit behavior therapy, or medication, or my and my husband's hard work, or even Caden's maturity. All of those things do help (in an inconsistent way) but each one of those things has also completely failed us at some point. The interesting thing about the teachers' comments is not that there was an absence of ADHD—there was peace within it.

I have no delusions that we cracked a code and can now sit back and watch our child effortlessly succeed in life. The teenage years have already thrown us several curveballs. In desperate moments I reference Jesus's five tips and focus on what I can do, releasing anything else to God.

Tip 1. Have Faith and Believe.
Tip 2. Do Not Be Afraid. Do Not Weep.
Tip 3. Persistently Advocate for Your Child.
Tip 4. Lift Up Your Child.
Tip 5. Go Your Way.

Jesus gave us a promise. *"... I am with you always ..."* Matthew 28:20 (NKJV) Jesus has been there for me at every point of my parenting journey—even before I asked him to be. As I look back to the turning point of my desperate parent story, I realize it was exactly that; a question I asked in desperation. "Jesus, how would you raise my kid?" My answer was right there in the question. *Raise* him. Lift him up.

Made in the USA
Monee, IL
18 November 2021